Preventing Workplace Meltdown:
An Employer's Guide to Maintaining a Psychologically Safe Workplace

A Carswell Implementation Guide

Martin Shain, S.J.D. and
Mary Ann Baynton, M.S.W., R.S.W.

CARSWELL®

ISBN 978-0-7798-3640-6

A cataloguing record for this publication is available from Library and Archives Canada.

Printed in Canada by Thomson Reuters.

Composition: Computer Composition of Canada Inc.

THOMSON REUTERS

CARSWELL, A DIVISION OF THOMSON REUTERS CANADA LIMITED

One Corporate Plaza
2075 Kennedy Road
Toronto, Ontario
M1T 3V4

Customer Relations
Toronto 1-416-609-3800
Elsewhere in Canada/U.S. 1-800-387-5164
Fax 1-416-298-5082
www.carswell.com
Online www.carswell.com/email

PREFACE

Sitting in a little café just beyond the property of the Centre for Addiction and Mental Health, Martin and Mary Ann decided that there was benefit in combining his perspective on the legal imperative to provide a psychologically safe work environment with strategies and stories that came from actual experiences she had as a consultant in the field of workplace mental health. By sharing the worst case scenario—being held legally liable for causing mental injury to an employee—along with the successful approaches used by others, it would be possible to learn what to avoid as well as practical strategies to prevent problems.

We have often heard people refer to emotional outbursts as meltdowns. They may happen because of untreated mental health issues such as depression or anxiety-related disorders. They may happen because of chronic stress or pressure. Or they may happen because of sudden and unexpected trauma or distress. In most cases, with a focus on wellness and balance, meltdowns can be prevented. We borrowed the term to refer to the experience that can happen in a workplace that is psychologically unsafe. It speaks to the effect of mental injuries on employees, loss of morale, reduction in productivity, damage to reputation that can affect recruitment and retention and, in many cases, a loss of profitability. A workplace meltdown is a negative result from failing to assess, address and abate psychological risk in the workplace.

Writing this book while we were both engaged in full-time work was a challenge that was made easier by those who helped us out. First and foremost is Martin's wife and business partner, Christine, who spent considerable time helping to bring Martin's careful, academic voice and Mary Ann's stream of consciousness approach to writing into a more cohesive book. Next would be Mary Ann's family who tolerated her sneaking away to McMaster University to write in seclusion in between her many business trips. And thanks also to Sheila and Neil at Carswell who helped us put it all together.

Finally, we wish to thank those organizations who graciously shared their work for the benefit of our readers as well as employees and employers across Canada. These include the Mental Health Commission of Canada, Guarding Minds at Work, Mental Health Works and the Great-West Life Centre for Mental Health in the Workplace.

From a little café to workplaces everywhere, our hope is that this book will help to prevent workplace meltdown and therefore prevent the resulting pain and distress that occurs in the aftermath.

INTRODUCTION

This book is about mental injuries in the workplace—what they are, how to assess the risks of their occurrence, how to reduce or prevent legal liability for them and how to create psychologically safe workplaces.

Mental injury at work has become a recognized category of harm in the law over the last 15 years and every year it becomes more important for employers to understand what it is and how to prevent it.

Damages for mental injury are reaching unprecedented levels. It is becoming easier for employees to find remedies through an increasing number of legal routes.

In addition to having damages awarded against them, employers are being faced with systemic orders from tribunals and commissions that are ever more invasive of management rights in the interests of reducing the risk of mental injuries at their source. And the source of such injuries is often identified by the law as predictably harmful ways of organizing, designing and directing the workplace.

Of course, the law does come up with solutions and remedies. But they are highly imperfect. We base the advice you will find here on the premise that no employer, union or HR professional actively wants to get ensnared in legal actions concerning the violation of a worker's mental health.

It can be ugly, expensive, ineffective and massively disruptive to the work of an organization, not to mention stressful, dispiriting and demoralizing for all involved.

In the following chapters, narratives derived from the law illustrate these observations and attempt to clarify what mental injury is and how it comes about.

The narratives are followed by commentaries entitled *Suggested Strategies* that propose ways in which these situations may have evolved differently had appropriate interventions and decisions been made along the way. Supplementing these commentaries are accounts from the field entitled *Workplace Interventions*, outside of the legal context, where interventions have been made as a result of calls for help from troubled workplaces.

Finally, to summarize, there are some basic principles and practices that have demonstrated potential to help employers create psychologically safe workplaces.

The last chapter will contain a discussion of the development of national standards for the assessment and abatement of psychological hazards in Canada and describe how this will help employers in their own efforts to create psychologically safe workplaces.

TABLE OF CONTENTS

CHAPTER 1

Mental Injury and the Psychologically Safe Workplace:
Emerging Legal Concepts

Occupational health and safety was once an unfamiliar concept to the majority of workplaces in Canada. Until the passage of Workers' Compensation Acts in the late 19th and early 20th centuries, redress for physically injured workers depended upon the willingness of the courts to entertain actions brought by individual workers or their bereaved families. The outcome of such actions was notoriously unpredictable. Little attention was paid to preventing injuries or ensuring safety except through the provisions of rudimentary legislation.

Today workers' right to safe working conditions is a commonly held value in practice and in law. Joint health and safety committees in larger organizations and an appointed health and safety representative in most smaller organizations are charged with identifying hazards and reducing risks to employees. The focus of their work is largely on physical health and safety issues. Organizations such as workers' compensation, labour unions, and health & safety associations offer substantial support and information in these areas.

Over the past 25 years or so, these organizations, other interested stakeholders and agencies such as the Mental Health Commission of Canada have begun to look deeper into issues of stress, burnout, mental illness and trauma caused in whole or in part by workplace conditions.

The concept of mental or psychological injury in the workplace has emerged much more slowly and only now stands alongside physical injury as a legitimate category of harm for which damages and other forms of remedy may be awarded.

This has happened not only as a result of developments in tort law, contract law, occupational health and safety, human rights, labour law, workers' compensation and employment standards, but also in the very way the law defines the employment relationship. One hundred and fifty years ago the employment contract was not seen as a relationship at all. It was a cut and dried commercial contract for the simple exchange of wages for labour. Today employment is seen as a relationship that evolves over time and accrues to its participants an increasingly complex body of rights and duties that include, but go far beyond this simple exchange.

Today, according to the Supreme Court of Canada, the Common Law contract of employment contains implied terms for psychological comfort based on what was assumed to be in the contemplation of the parties at the time the bargain was struck.[1] Unless these implied terms for psychological comfort are deliberately deleted in a written employment contract these terms stand as a basis upon which actions for breach of contract can be advanced. It remains to be seen how extensive the protection offered by the assurance of psychological comfort actually is. Nevertheless it appears from the Supreme Court's reasoning that most employment contracts would be presumed to include at least some protection against the gratuitous infliction of mental suffering during the course of the employment relationship and including its termination.

In labour law—the law dealing with unionized employees—the end result is similar, but for different reasons based on how collective agreements are deemed to include provisions for the protection of mental health.

For these reasons alone it appears very unlikely that the trend toward legal recognition of a right to have one's mental health at work protected in some basic ways will be turned back.

---

[1]   See the *Fidler* case in Martin Shain, *Stress, Mental Injury and the Law in Canada* (2009), <www.mentalhealthcommission.ca> at 37-39.

This and other developments in the law combine to present employers with new duties of care—the duty to provide a psychologically safe workplace and the consequent duty to prevent foreseeable mental injuries.

The *duty to provide a psychologically safe workplace* means making every reasonable effort to protect the mental health of employees. More precisely, it means being vigilant for and rectifying instances of negligent, reckless and intentional conduct that could foreseeably lead to mental injury.

Mental injury is the realization of risk to employee mental health that results from negligent, reckless and intentional acts or omissions on the part of employers, their agents and other employees and frequently takes the form of debilitating anxiety, depression and burnout. It is not, however, the same as mental illness although it may amount to the same thing sometimes. The difference is that according to the law in Canada as it stands today, mental injury is more allied to any significant impact on mental health that leads to a chronic inability to function as usual at work or at home.

How big is the risk?

As an employer, or as someone with responsibilities for keeping the organization out of trouble, you may ask, why worry about the risk of legal actions involving mental injury when those risks are very remote? Do we not have more pressing concerns?

The answer to this question depends on how we define the risk of legal action.

If we define the risk as the probability of being hauled before the Supreme Court of Canada after years of battling through the lower courts then the risk is very small: a bit like the risk of being hit by lightning twice in the same day.

But if we define risk as the odds of being involved in conflicts, grievances or complaints which divert energy from the business of the organization and that harbour the express or implied threat of some form of legal action, then it becomes a lot more real and immediate. In fact many organizations experience threats at this level on a fairly routine basis. For others, the risk is manifested in high turnover rates, low productivity and/or an inability to recruit and retain talent.

Some workplaces are intrinsically more susceptible to such threats than others for a number of reasons, including the nature of the business, composition of the workforce and the availability of remedies (which vary across the country).

However one of the biggest sources of exposure to threat of legal action is the way work is assigned, organized and managed.

If we characterize workplaces according to this variable, it is clear how some are "psychologically safe" (unlikely to generate mental injuries) while others are the opposite: "psychologically unsafe" (quite likely to generate mental injuries).

The psychological safety of a workplace refers to the way in which it manages the risk of careless, negligent, reckless and intentional injury to the mental health of its employees. Significant mental harm rarely results from a single bad day or inappropriate remark. Rather it is more often ongoing behaviours or conditions that should have been foreseen as potentially causing harm.

To put it another way, a psychologically safe workplace is one in which every practical effort is made to protect the mental health of employees from acts and omissions (particularly, but not exclusively, those of managers and supervisors) that a reasonable person would anticipate leading to significant mental harm.

If psychologically safe workplaces can be described as *green*, and psychologically unsafe workplaces as *red*, then the odds of conflict and legal action are at least 30% higher in red than in green organizations. (The last chapter will help you determine which category your workplace falls into.)

While some form of legal action might be seen as arising in one out of ten green workplaces, it will be seen in four out of ten red workplaces.

The law sets the scene for conflict by providing a framework within which it is increasingly possible and practical to claim financial and systemic remedies for assaults upon one's mental health. And these remedies are multiplying in our society.

The good news is that the law provides numerous accounts that help observant employers and managers find ways to avoid trouble and steer a course toward low conflict, psychologically safe work environments.

In addition, the lessons to be learned from these accounts have economic value because low conflict, psychologically safe workplaces are also more efficient, productive and competitive.[2]

There are numerous methods of categorizing the stories that we can extract from the law as it relates to mental health and mental injury in the workplace. Some methods are technical and are based on the ways in which legal actions are framed and advanced. For example, they could be classified according to the branch of law under which they were brought

---

[2]   For key references, see: <www.guardingmindsatwork.ca>.

forward—such as human rights, workers' compensation, torts, contracts, grievances, occupational health and safety, employment standards, etc. This more technical analysis has been published elsewhere.[3]

Alternatively, these narratives could be organized according to the stage of the employment relationship at which the legal action arises. For example, we could address discipline and discharge, return to work and accommodation.

However our experience and analysis tell us that regardless of how legal actions arise and are framed, all of them involve, in one way or another, failures in three key areas of responsibility:

1. **failure to make reasonable and clear job demands;**
2. **failure to make it safe for employees to voice their work-related or personal concerns;**
3. **failure to monitor and respond to contentious situations among employees.**

Each set of responsibilities will be explored in the next three chapters.

These chapters contain descriptions of legal cases that emerged from workplaces in which judges, arbitrators and commissioners found that some of these responsibilities were *not* met—with dire results.

These are followed by case histories of workplace interventions where these responsibilities and duties were addressed with positive results for both the worker and the organization.

---

[3] Martin Shain, *Stress, Mental Injury and the Law in Canada* (2009), a discussion paper for the Mental Health Commission of Canada. This report is an analysis of Canadian jurisprudence as it relates to remedies for mental injury in the workplace. See also: Martin Shain, *Tracking the Perfect Legal Storm, an update to Stress, Mental Injury and the Law in Canada* (2010). Both reports are available in French and English at: <www.mentalhealthcommission.ca>.

The divisions between the three sets of responsibilities are not watertight and overlap in many instances. Nevertheless all three together form *imperatives for managing the workplace in such a way that mental health is protected.* Although it is important for employers to set objectives or targets within each of them as distinct areas, they are interdependent. Progress in one area is likely to depend on progress in the other two. They are best seen as three lines of advance in a single strategy to achieve a psychologically safe workplace.

In the following three chapters these three areas of responsibility dominate the narrative that emerges from case law and the consultative experience. The term "responsibility" refers to obligations that are largely *discretionary,* but which, if not fulfilled, can fail to meet certain *legal* duties that have implications for liability. Meeting the responsibilities described here is a *prerequisite* for the discharge of certain legal duties. So while the law cannot address the failure of these responsibilities as such, it can and does condemn the *results* of this failure.

These responsibilities are mostly relevant to the conduct of the employment relationship *while it is still intact.* We do not deal, except incidentally, with mental injury that may occur primarily as a result of how workers are fired since this is an area with which most employers are already quite familiar and where the case law is relatively settled.

Mental injury that occurs during the course of the employment relationship, and the means to prevent it, are far less understood.

For all practical purposes, this means that in order to fulfil the duty to provide a psychologically safe workplace the essential areas of responsibilities must themselves be effectively addressed.

Our aim, in this book, is to provide employers with practical guidance that will help them understand and discharge these responsibilities and duties more effectively. In the predictable future, our advice will be supported by national standards for the assessment and abatement of risks to psychological safety in the workplace and these are presently being developed. These standards are the subject of the final chapter of this book.

The Psychologically Safe Workplace: Key Responsibilities and Duties

Seen as a whole, the three sets of responsibilities described below are essentially different aspects of the *super-duty* to provide a psychologically safe workplace that has emerged from several branches of Canadian law during the last 10 years.

At its simplest, this duty is to assess and address modifiable risks to employee mental health arising in whole or in part from the ways in which work is organized, assigned, designed and managed.

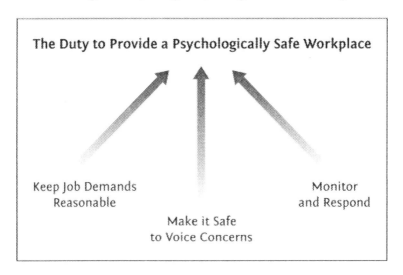

The Duty to Provide a Psychologically Safe Workplace

Keep Job Demands
Reasonable

Make it Safe
to Voice Concerns

Monitor
and Respond

Basic Responsibilities Supporting the Duty

1. Keep job demands reasonable and adjust them to individual capacities

Employers are responsible for determining what excessive and unreasonable demands mean in relation to individual employees and for taking appropriate steps to adjust the situation where required.

This responsibility is more readily discharged when judicious efforts are made to select employees who are right for the job in the first place: when choosing candidates for a position both the physical and psychological demands of a job should be considered, especially where the position requires management or support of workers.

Hiring or promoting that is done on the basis of technical skills alone can lead to the placement of employees into situations where they do not have the skills to recognize when their demands are too high and are causing undue stress or hardship. Similarly, when a person who is hired for a position of authority is unaware of the necessity for making their expectations and instructions clear, the result can be ongoing distress for subordinates who must operate in an atmosphere of uncertainty or chaos. Interpersonal competence among supervisors and managers can make a significant contribution to a psychologically safe work environment.

The reasonableness of job demands becomes even more important for employees who are experiencing mental disability or disorder, including depression and anxiety-related illnesses. Employees with mental health challenges who remain on the job and those who are returning after absences may be particularly vulnerable to insensitive or unreasonable demands. Communication styles may need to be adjusted and accommodation made to the particular challenges or barriers that the current mental health of the returning worker presents.

Failure to meet these obligations which results in mental injury can be construed as failure to meet fundamental requirements of the legal duty to provide a psychologically safe workplace, leading to liability in several potential areas.

2. Make it safe to speak up

There is a responsibility to create an atmosphere of basic trust in which workers who report to you or for whom you have obligations feel safe in declaring problematic situations, circumstances and conditions which are affecting, or might affect their job performance or well-being at work. This includes the responsibility to learn about critical vulnerabilities among your workers, including health issues.

It is not uncommon for courts and tribunals to find that an employer knew or ought to have known that an employee was struggling with mental health issues. In such instances, courts and tribunals may hold that the employer should have offered disability coverage rather than terminating the employee and they may order compensation on this basis.

Turning a blind eye to distress or the failure to notice an obvious situation is typically regarded with disapproval by courts and tribunals in cases of mental injury.

The responsibility to facilitate a workplace environment that encourages employees to feel safe to speak out about their concerns without fear of retaliation, ridicule or being ignored requires that those in positions of authority have the required skills.

Failure to meet these responsibilities can lead to a subsequent failure to adequately discharge the legal duty to accommodate workers with mental disabilities or disorders up to a reasonable standard when

required. This duty can be seen as a subcategory of the super-duty to provide a psychologically safe workplace.

3. Monitor and Respond to Contentious Issues

Employers must be aware of, and take proactive steps to amend situations of interpersonal conflict that could foreseeably give rise to mental injury. Often, human resources personnel or senior management claim to have been unaware of ongoing conflict among workers or between a worker and supervisor. But ignorance is not an excuse in the eyes of the law.

It is important that organizations have procedures in place to ensure that a psychologically safe workplace is the norm, which includes hiring supervisors and managers who have interpersonal skills.

If failure to meet these obligations leads to mental injury, the door is opened to employer liability on a number of fronts. Monitoring and responding to such warning signs is a fundamental aspect of the super-duty to provide a psychologically safe workplace.

An important note on the cases

All the legal cases that we refer to are a small sample of a much larger body of case law.

They were chosen to demonstrate *typical, recurring workplace situations* that can easily give rise to legal actions.

Not all types of legal action are illustrated here. No meaning or significance should be attached to the choice of cases used here beyond their value as examples of what can happen when mental injury arises in the workplace.

By their very nature, legal cases refer to workplaces and individuals by name. But in telling the stories from these selected cases, we are not in any way trying to assign blame. In fact, the sad truth is that almost any workplace can get ensnared in legal webs involving mental injury. In other words, it could happen to *any* employer.

These examples are to help you understand when mental injury may occur and develop strategies or approaches to reduce risk in your workplace.

The Role of Employee (Family) Assistance Plans or E(F)APs in creating and maintaining a Psychologically Safe Workplace.

There is a common, **though incorrect**, assumption that if an employer has provided an Employee (Family) Assistance Plan, the duty to provide a psychologically safe workplace has been discharged.

It is important to note that while E(F)APs can play an integral role in *maintaining* a psychologically safe workplace as we have defined it, they are not in themselves the primary means of *creating* one. They are a necessary but not sufficient component of a comprehensive strategy for creating and sustaining a psychologically safe workplace.

Essentially and by their nature E(F)APs are *after the fact* (downstream) interventions, while the imperatives of the psychologically safe workplace are on the *prevention* (upstream) end of the continuum.

Employee (and Family) Assistance Plans (E(F)APs or EAPs) are valuable resources that provide consultation services for individual employees and sometimes their family members who may be struggling with a wide variety of issues including problems and conflicts that arise in home and workplace environments, financial concerns, addictions, child care and elder care.

While these services have the potential to address and improve problematic situations that impact employee mental health, it is important to understand that few, if any E(F)AP services in themselves diagnose or treat mental illnesses.

If the automatic response to employees who appear to be struggling is to refer them to the E(F)AP, it may not result in their getting the help they really need, nor in an improvement of performance or behaviour in the workplace. In ambiguous or very difficult cases a recommended approach for employers who procure the services of E(F)AP providers is to confer with the providers on how best to handle the situation when mental health problems are suspected. Assessments or referrals could be done by the E(F)AP service, but there might also be alternative approaches involving referral to community services or discussions with medical professionals. It is important to be clear about what is and is not provided by the E(F)AP.

Most E(F)AP providers offer services to supervisors and managers who are struggling with employee performance or behaviour issues. Being able to pick up the phone and get advice from a knowledgeable professional which addresses these issues as they are happening can be of great value, but only if supervisors and managers are aware of the service. Even organizations that have human resources available for this purpose will recognize that managers do not always want to admit their frustration or to expose the situation to those in upper management. Timely use of a confidential E(F)AP service can prevent smaller problems from becoming larger problems that have to be brought to the attention of leaders in the organization.

CHAPTER 2

The Duty to Provide a Psychologically Safe Workplace: Keeping Demands within Reason

Excessive or unreasonable job demands contribute significantly to work conditions that give rise to mental injuries. Keeping job demands within reasonable bounds is a keystone of the duty to provide a psychologically safe workplace. The question, of course, is how do we determine what is reasonable when the answer may not be the same for every employee, even those doing the same job?

Frequently, job demands can become progressively less reasonable over a period of time. Neither the receiver nor the issuer of increased work demands may realize that a toxic situation is brewing until it boils over. By then, it may be too late to ward off serious consequences. The overwhelmed employee may conclude that he or she has sustained mental injury and bring some form of legal action against their employer.

Most of us have heard about the unusual behaviour of frogs in boiling water. If a frog is dropped into a pot of boiling water, it would hop right out if at all possible. When the water ever so slowly and gradually becomes hotter and hotter, most frogs do not seem to notice and will stay in until it is too late to escape. When subjected on a gradual basis to ever increasing demands and stress at work, workers may not speak up or try to escape until mental injury has occurred. Too little, too late!

Routine monitoring of workload and task distribution is central to avoiding such situations, but it is important to understand that perception of workload can be as damaging as the actual workload: sometimes perceived pressure to perform may be the source of harm rather than the actual work performed or required.

Multi-tasking as an effective way of getting things done has not performed as advertised, but it continues to be an approach encouraged in many workplaces. The human mind can only focus on one thing at a time and switching from one task to another repeatedly can actually diminish efficiency and productivity as the mind refocuses with each shift of attention.[1] If the stress from a conflicted situation, lack of recognition or control, and uncertainty or ambiguity about job requirements are added to this method of working, the ingredients for a psychologically unsafe environment are present. Such environments can contribute to a number of stress-based illnesses. Although variety and the flexibility to change tasks throughout the day are considered best practices for healthy job design, the ability to focus on a single task at a time without significant interruption can contribute to psychological safety as well as to productivity and quality control.

Working a regular eight hour day at any job where there is constant pressure, uncertainty or conflict can contribute to a perception of unreasonable or excessive job demands even when the hours of work are entirely normal. The unreasonableness or excessiveness in such instances lies in the emotional or psychological job strain associated with how the work is assigned, managed or supervised.

Here are three examples of how excessive, unreasonable job demands were found to have led or contributed to mental injuries. After each example, strategies that may help to prevent or mitigate this type of risk, often taken from real-life intervention cases, are described.

---

[1] D. Crenshaw, *The Myth of Multi-tasking. How "doing it all" gets nothing done* (Jossey Bass, 2008).

THE CASE OF THE ANGRY TRUCK DRIVER

WHAT HAPPENED?

This is a case about a long distance truck driver who died of a heart attack after a period of severe emotional and physical stress. It is a claim for survivor benefits brought by his family. The initial claim failed and this is the result of the appeal from that decision.[2]

The driver had been exposed to hot, humid and cramped working conditions for a weekend when he was cooped up in his truck, far from home, waiting to make a delivery the following Monday.

He was angry and frustrated with his employer for sending him to a destination where they *knew* he would arrive too late to make the delivery and knew he would have to wait out the weekend in his truck.

He was forbidden to leave his truck for security reasons.

As a diabetic, he was unable to exercise the dietary controls necessary to maintain his health because of his limited ability to seek proper food. He also had pre-existing hypertension, kidney and gallbladder problems.

Shortly after this delivery was finally made, he suffered a fatal heart attack at another location on the return leg of his journey.

THE WORKERS' COMPENSATION APPEALS BOARD DECISION

Board policy allows entitlement to benefits for a work-related aggravation of a pre-existing heart condition, if the work-related aggravation consists of unusual physical exertion or acute emotional stress with no significant delay in the onset of symptoms.

---

[2] Decision No. 851/09, (2009), 2009 ONWSIAT 2309, 2009 CarswellOnt 7601 (Ont. W.S.I.A.T.).

The Tribunal accepted a medical expert witness' conclusion as follows:

> It is clear that he [the driver] had cardiovascular death and it is clear that his risk factor, especially diabetes, played a major role. I think it is also very probable that the stresses he was under at the time or just before his death played a role in precipitating the event, especially driving in a bad storm, high temperature and humidity leading to dehydration, his anxiety over his diabetic control, and his anger. These stresses all led to a change in equilibrium of his clotting system, which likely resulted in thrombosis of one of his coronary arteries or a cardiac arrhythmia leading to his death.
>
> My conclusion is that he almost certainly had pre-existing cardiovascular disease but this long trip led to anger and anxiety and inability to control his diabetes, which were all precipitating factors in his sudden death.

WHAT COULD HAVE BEEN DONE DIFFERENTLY?

Clearly getting this load to its destination was very important to the driver's employer, but was it so important that he would have intentionally put a vulnerable employee in harm's way? For otherwise healthy employees, this situation may have been a bit annoying, but it would not likely have been fatal.

How is an employer to know if objections from employees about their work are significant or simply require some persistence and determination on their part to get the job done?

No employer wants to "give in" at every complaint, but neither do most employers want to cause harm. The two approaches described below may help employers decide whether job demands are unreasonable or excessive in a given situation with a particular employee.

Suggested Strategies #1
Engage all stakeholders in planning

The first approach is to have a work environment where tasks, assignments and instructions are discussed rather than simply distributed: "the participative approach." In the participative approach, all relevant stakeholders are engaged in decisions about how the work gets done, especially work that requires extra employee effort and commitment. The best solutions are most often achieved in this way and crisis situations are more likely to be averted.

If there are problems with a particular project or approach, a conversation and shared understanding up front can avoid a lot of hostility and difficulties down the road. This is true both in individual assignments and team work.

In the *Case of the Angry Truck Driver*, a load needed to be delivered to an important client. Relevant stakeholders might have included shipping, sales, dispatch and the trucker. If these stakeholders had been involved from the first in determining together how this load was to be delivered, given the trucker's health issues, they might have identified in advance the challenges involved in sending this man on this particular trip. They would have had the opportunity to develop strategies so that the load could have been delivered without undue health risk to the driver.

What were the options? Could another worker at the delivery location have dropped off an appropriate meal or relieved the driver for a few hours? With dispatch on board as part of the solution, might this load have been switched with another driver who did not have the same health issues? Could arrangements have been made to park the load in a secure area near the delivery site so the driver could leave the vehicle for a time? Was it possible for sales to negotiate a later date for the delivery?

The issue is not that employees should determine what is to be done, but that there are often reasonable options on how the work is to be accomplished that address the needs of all stakeholders. However, these options take some flexibility and creativity in the organizational structure to allow them to develop. These options can then be considered by those in leadership positions who are balancing broader business criteria including economic realities, competing demands, organizational effectiveness and reputation as it impacts sales, recruitment and retention.

> **Whenever possible, engage all stakeholders in planning how work will be done once it has been determined what measurable outcomes are required. This can improve commitment, clarity of role expectations and quality of work, while identifying possible challenges and obstacles.**

In some organizations, providing departments that will eventually be involved in joint projects, with the opportunity for an ongoing exchange of views *early* in the decision making process tends to reduce the "silo" effect. While managing by consensus could be paralyzing and even disastrous for some organizations, encouraging early input from teams and individuals, who will soon have a role in upcoming work, can improve both commitment from individuals and quality of work. If the organization or leadership is clear on what outcomes are required, seeking input from all stakeholders on *how* they can be achieved can reduce unexpected challenges or obstacles.

Workplace Interventions: Accounts from the field #1

An organization whose departments had traditionally operated in "silos" was initially unconvinced that the participative approach would work. Most departments felt that their own teams worked hard and did good work, but the other departments did not work as hard or contribute as much. They did not work together on projects. By having different perspectives on priorities, approaches and results, the departments often competed with each other for resources and caused bottlenecks in work flow.

A new manager, who had been exposed to a different approach in her previous work environment, was tasked with a project that would cross over several departments before completion. When she asked the other departments to sit down with her before the project began, to hear her plans and provide feedback, they were sceptical. They needed to be encouraged to speak up and feel safe enough to offer their views, but eventually they did.

Not only was the project completed with much less delay than the organization was used to, but also the various departments began to develop respect for the knowledge, expertise and effort put forward by the others. The project was the first of its kind for the organization and won an award for excellence. It began a new approach of cross-collaboration and involvement of stakeholders in the planning processes.

Suggested Strategies #2
Not "No!" ... but "Why?"

Often the employer's or manager's first impulse to a job demand that appears unreasonable, excessive or impractical is to respond impatiently with a negative remark or to fall back on an explanation about why the conventional way is the best or only possible way.

But what if a discussion with the employee aimed at understanding the basis of the employee's request or objections could produce a better resolution?

Rather than dismiss the concerns of the employee who had a complaint, the person in a managerial or supervisory capacity might respond by asking a few questions: "What would make this better for you?" "Why does this cause you difficulties?" "What do you think would be a better approach?" Instead of a stalemate, these questions can be the first steps in an attempt to discover alternatives to the current situation and its challenges.

The following scenario illustrates the value of this alternate approach.

Workplace Interventions: Accounts from the field #2

The employee was emphatic in his declaration that he needed to have the corner office to accommodate his disability. Unfortunately this was the Vice-President's office and at first glance it seemed absurd to suggest that this much more junior employee might bump him out. Instead of having his request met with astonishment or ridicule, he was asked why the corner office would accommodate his disability. He shared that he had Seasonal Affective Disorder (S.A.D.) and the doctor had advised that he maximize his exposure to natural light during the winter months. All employees were in cubicles without windows except the Vice-President and President who occupied the two corner offices. The request for an office with windows was reasonable when the underlying rationale was disclosed, although still impractical.

In the discussion that developed there was a sincere attempt to meet this employee's requirement for natural light. As the man began to understand that the seriousness of his condition was appreciated by the company, he also entered into the brainstorming process. He offered a couple of solutions. He had heard about special lamps that simulated natural light and had proven effective for S.A.D. Alternatively, he suggested that if he could move to a cubicle on the perimeter of the room where a window was placed, removing one panel of the cubicle would expose him to sufficient light. Although this would leave him with less privacy and quiet, he felt it was worth the exposure to sunlight. Had the employee's request for a corner office been dismissed with a negative response he may have felt that his right to reasonable accommodation was violated or that he was not valued.

> **Before saying no to a request or suggestion, ask why the person feels this is important or valuable. You may find that the underlying rationale or need leads to an alternative solution that is a win-win.**

The advantages of the consultative approach for management

Many in management believe that engaging in this type of dialogue with employees will lead to spurious requests over minor issues and result in chaotic conditions. This approach does not require agreement that everything will change to suit individual preferences. It does mean that challenges from employees should be given consideration as worthy inquiries that might lead to alternative solutions that solve work-related or performance issues. A conversation with a complainant that goes along the lines of, "You may be right. I was not looking at it from that perspective. Help me understand what you consider a better approach to be that would meet our (or your) work objectives," can produce effective solutions to situations that otherwise might spiral into serious conflicts.

Complaining for the sake of complaining can be kept to a minimum by requiring complainants to engage in solutions to their own problems. When the manager responds to their complaints with enquiries such as, "Why is that a problem for you?" or "What would you like to do about that?" employees know that raising objections will lead to an invitation to seek a reasonable solution.

It also helps managers and supervisors avoid the pitfall of repeatedly "rescuing employees" from situations that will likely continue to occur until real change in the workplace happens as a result of the employee's own change in behaviour or attitude.

The individual, in working towards the solution, may self-correct to agree with the original rationale for a workplace situation or find an alternative that actually works. The employer, manager, or supervisor has avoided dismissing the complainant's concern by simply saying "no," has empowered the employee to consider alternative solutions and together they have found the one that they agree is best.

THE CASE OF THE HARRIED ACCOUNT MANAGER

WHAT HAPPENED?

The plaintiff in this case, Susanne Zorn-Smith, had worked 21 years for a bank. She was by all accounts a diligent, loyal, compliant and well-liked employee.

She had moved around the region a lot, at the bank's request, and worked extremely long hours in spite of having a young family at home.

She would often return to work after dinner and sometimes worked on Sundays, not because she was incompetent, but because she was diligent in the extreme.

There came a point, after some years of trying to upgrade her skills, where she began to burn-out. The demands of the job were exacerbated by ongoing training requirements to formally qualify for the managerial position that she already occupied.

She succumbed to one episode of depressive illness, then eventually to another, on the basis of which she was placed on disability leave.

After several weeks, while still on leave, the bank gave her an ultimatum: either come back to work in her former managerial position, come back part-time in a junior position, or do not come back at all. She declined to return, and the bank dismissed her.

She sued for wrongful dismissal, the intentional infliction of mental distress, loss of disability benefits and punitive damages for callous disregard.

One of Ms. Zorn-Smith's key supervisors testified that he had no idea of the negative effect the severe stress of the workplace, particularly that associated with chronic, severe understaffing was having on her.

He was found to have trivialized her health concerns, which she brought to him on numerous occasions.

The Court noted the testimony of the plaintiff's physician that she was sleep-deprived, exhausted, irritable and burnt-out.

This physician (whose testimony clashed with that of the bank's own doctor) opined that the solution to the problem was to provide the plaintiff with adequate study time and to have realistic expectations for her with regard to her current level of training, a view that the Court appears to have accepted, further characterizing the employer's lack of concern for the plaintiff's health as "reckless."

There was a notable lack of support from the plaintiff's superiors with regard to technical matters.

Her marriage began to suffer, and finally she was diagnosed as having "an adjustment disorder with depressed and anxious mood" (the technical term for burn out). Her physician saw this result as a workplace issue, rather than as a personal issue, with regard to potential solutions.

By this stage, Ms. Zorn-Smith had "loss of appetite, memory loss, lack of concentration, mood swings, exhaustion, a loss of self-worth and a loss of self-esteem ...[and] she was angry and impatient."

In her physician's view, this amounted to total incapacitation. He made frequent reference to the "excessive demands" to which she was subjected and to the "disastrous" consequences of the employer's proposal that she return to work part-time: "it will translate into being paid half as much to do three times as much."

Ms. Zorn-Smith told her supervisor in the context of refusing the bank's final offer that returning to an unmodified workplace "would kill her. She felt mistreated, abused and forced out because of unreasonable job requirements."

The Court determined that the plaintiff was terminated without cause, given that she was legitimately on disability leave at the time of her dismissal.[3]

The judge said,

> I find that Ms. Zorn-Smith continued to suffer from exhaustion, poor concentration, an inability to think straight, lack of confidence and self-doubt to the extent that she could not have functioned in the role of Financial Services Manager, or for that matter, in any other role at the Bank."

> Her energy, initiative and stamina had been drained out of her by too many months of unreasonable work demands relating not only to the normal work day but also nights and weekends.

In weighing the evidence concerning the role of plaintiff's domestic situation in her burn out, the Court dismissed the bank's contention that

---

[3]   *Zorn-Smith v. Bank of Montreal*, (2003), 2003 CarswellOnt 4845, [2003] O.J. No. 5044 (Ont. S.C.J.).

this was the real cause of her problem. Indeed, "there was nothing in the evidence to suggest that Ms. Zorn-Smith could not cope with everything, had her work demands been within some reasonable parameters. They simply were not. ... I find that Ms. Zorn-Smith's adjustment disorder with depressed and anxious mood was caused predominantly by unreasonable work demands and not by family stresses."

Later the Court noted, "It was the responsibility of the Bank to ensure a safe workplace for its employees, a workplace that was not making them ill and unable to work."

The Court also noted that

> Ms. Zorn-Smith had worked for the Bank since she was 15, and her father had been a Vice President of the Bank until his death. She was devoted to the Bank, and considered the Bank employees her family. The multitude of feelings which she would have experienced upon not being supported by the Bank in regard to her continuing disability and then being terminated from the Bank could not help but to have compounded her feelings of loss and inadequacy, and to have hindered her normal functioning.

The Court held that the bank's behaviour in the manner of dismissal was unfair and in bad faith justifying a longer notice period (in this case, damages in lieu). The Court entertained "no doubt that the way in which Ms. Zorn-Smith was treated at the time of her dismissal worsened her psychological state."

The Court further characterized the plaintiff's lack of confidence in her own ability to function as a foreseeable result of the bank's improper actions.

With regard to the claim for damages in connection with intentional infliction of mental distress, the Court held that reckless disregard of consequences is sufficient to meet the legal criteria where the elements to be proven are:

1. flagrant or outrageous conduct;
2. calculated to produce harm; and
3. resulting in a visible and provable illness.

The Court held that the tort of intentional infliction of mental suffering was proven because:

- the bank *knew* that plaintiff was exhausted and worn out as a result of chronic understaffing;

- the bank was *well aware* that the plaintiff suffered burn out on a previous occasion (2000), requiring a short leave of absence;

- supervisors *knew* that the plaintiff had been requesting relief from her workload;

- despite this knowledge, the bank continued to reduce staffing levels, thus increasing the workload on plaintiff;

- despite the plaintiff's *pleas for relief*, the bank continued to keep on the pressure;

- the bank *knew* of her history of long hours and missed lunches;

- the bank took advantage of plaintiff's generous nature "in total disregard to" the toll its demands were taking on her health, and the health of her family" [emphasis added].

The Court concluded,

> This callous disregard for the health of an employee was flagrant and outrageous. That Susanne Zorn-Smith would suffer a further burnout was predictable—the only question was when it would come. It was foreseeable that such a burnout would cause her mental suffering. I

find that the Bank's conduct was the primary cause of Susanne Zorn-Smith's adjustment disorder with depressed and anxious mood.

However, the Court did not award punitive damages because the elements of malice and oppression were not present.

WHAT COULD HAVE BEEN DONE DIFFERENTLY?

The significant legal principles in this case have been italicized in the preceding narrative to help them stand out. They amount to the proposition that where harm to employee mental health is reasonably foreseeable and there is a duty of care to provide a safe system of work, the employer or its agents may be liable for such harm.

The law usually recognizes reasonable foreseeability when "everyone knows" that work demands are too unreasonable and that they pose a threat to health.

The *Case of the Harried Account Manager* relies heavily on community standards to define what constitutes unreasonable demands and what is reasonably foreseeable. It tells us that in Common Law the duty of care to provide a safe system of work embraces a duty to avoid reasonably foreseeable harm to the emotional or mental health of employees.

This case is about a good employee whose distress was ignored and trivialized by management. Most employers would look at this and say they would never disregard such obvious suffering on the part of a valued employee and therefore the story is not relevant to them.

But the irony is that the bank in question was, and is, a well-respected employer recognized and acknowledged for its state of the art human resources policies and approach to health promotion.

There is a simple message here: mental injury resulting from excessive work demands can occur even in the best regulated workplaces if a high level of vigilance is not maintained.

Once identified and acknowledged, the challenge of perceived work overload can be approached in much the same way as described in the *Case of the Angry Truck Driver*. As in that situation, the issues raised in the *Case of the Harried Account Manager* required discussion among all the concerned parties.

Perceived excessive or unreasonable workload on the part of one employee can often signal the need to review workload distribution issues in the team or unit as a whole.

Often, these reviews, conducted in the open-minded, non-judgemental way described in the commentary on the case of the angry trucker, reveal that workload is an issue not only for the person complaining, but also for other members of the team.

Frequently, it turns out that there is a more general or systemic concern about the way work is distributed and how the team functions as a whole. A common occurrence is that various members of the unit or team feel that they are working harder than others, that others are not pulling their weight, and that this is not fair. These shared negative perceptions are often a breeding ground for conflict and for the subsequent germination of legal actions.

How is the employee's personal health my responsibility as an employer?

This is a fair question. It's not up to employers or managers to diagnose, treat or counsel their workers. In fact, it is unethical for a person in a position of power over another to engage in a therapeutic relationship. This means that even if the manager happens to be qualified to diagnose, treat or counsel, it is not ethical to do so with an employee or direct report. It puts the employee or direct report in an untenable position— take the advice, or risk losing your boss' approval.

When the boss is not qualified to diagnose, treat or counsel, this becomes even more problematic in that what they perceive as good advice may in fact be detrimental to the well-being of the person they are giving it to. The focus in the workplace should be on offering advice about work-related issues only and providing access to qualified resources to assist with health or personal issues. This approach helps to prevent the well-intentioned and over-involved manager from inadvertently giving bad advice. It also relieves the emotionally incompetent manager of a responsibility he or she is not qualified to fulfill. In both cases, keeping the focus on helping the individual with work-related issues only helps avoid unintended consequences.

In the *Case of the Harried Account Manager* described above, solutions to some of the work-related challenges could have included managing training requirements differently, offering more support through student help or contract workers, reprioritizing tasks so that the employee did not see everything as having equal importance, removing all but essential duties until balance could be restored, or any number of other possibilities that could have been discussed.

This approach focuses on addressing the only things that are truly within the control and authority of supervisors or managers, namely, work-related factors.

Giving employees advice on managing their personal life or their health conditions in your capacity as an employer is to be avoided at all costs.

Of course, it is also not reasonable to think that every committed employee who chooses to work overtime is headed for a health crisis. Sometimes employees are simply passionate about their work or want to prove themselves so they can open the door to new opportunities.

In the context of strain due to working overtime, supervisors and managers who observe trends in energy and attitude in employees can help identify those who are struggling. If the person's energy and attitude remain fairly consistent, they're probably fine. If their energy is waning (or in some cases, such as bipolar disorder, *increasing* to unusual levels) or their attitude is shifting significantly over time, there may be an underlying issue. The only way to find out is to have a conversation with the individual that is rooted in concern for their well-being. It can begin with, "You don't seem to be yourself lately. I have noticed a decrease in energy or what looks like increased tension" or some other non-judgmental observation. Then it's best to stop and allow the employee a chance to share what he or she is experiencing. It may take several moments for them to decide if they feel safe in opening up, deciding what they will share, considering what might be done with the information or even thinking about what has actually changed for them lately. If the boss begins to offer his or her own suggestions or interpretations, it may interfere with this thought process and miss out on any opportunity to get at the real issue.

The boss should not be probing for personal information for its own sake and certainly not trying to make a diagnosis. He or she is discharging the responsibility to know enough about those who report to him or her in order to avoid doing them foreseeable harm.

In having this kind of conversation, the manager or supervisor can decide whether there is a need to intervene in restricting overtime or let the individual continue to work the extra hours. In any case, supervisors can let employees know that this extra work in the form of overtime is not required and that their health comes first. It may even be worthwhile to document this assertion on your part. Judges, arbitrators and commissioners are more likely to see this approach as reasonable, even if in the end the employee refuses your help.

What if the complaining worker was never an ideal employee?

The *Harried Account Manager* was a valued and loyal employee. If anything, she was too compliant for her own good. Nevertheless, instead of being helped to find workplace solutions, she had her concerns trivialized and she was humiliated and shamed for speaking out in a vain attempt to salvage her mental health.

But what if the employee is *not* exactly the most valued? What if his or her behaviour is difficult for co-workers to tolerate? Is it possible to use shaming techniques to bring about positive change? Does blame play a part in their taking responsibility for their own poor performance? How do you intervene when behaviours in the workplace are intolerable but where solutions are not clear cut?

Good Intentions Gone Bad: the Negative Impact of "Blame & Shame"

Interventions can sometimes go wrong and attempts to resolve conflict may worsen the situation. The following example of this type of negative outcome is the story of a female employee suffering with depression and severe anxiety whose behaviour had alienated her co-workers. An intervention was attempted.

Workplace Interventions: Accounts from the field

As part of the intervention, the consultant who had been hired asked all the workers to sit in a so-called "safe circle." Each of the co-workers was asked to share what it was about their co-worker with depression that irritated them. One by one the co-workers told stories about how this woman's behaviour affected them or pointed out her flaws while the woman sat, devastated and humiliated by what she heard. During the process some of those who spoke out in the circle were disturbed by the exercise. Afterwards, the woman and some of the co-workers claimed they were seriously traumatized by this experience. In addition, several workers complained to management that this intervention did not improve anything.

The consultant, on hearing complaints about the lack of positive outcome, brought the group back to the safe circle to talk about what they *valued* about this woman. However, by this point in the proceedings no one would agree to speak out because no one felt safe at all. The circle was disbanded, the woman went off on sick leave and it is uncertain if she will ever be able to return. A few of her colleagues now struggle with their own anxiety.

As a tool for intervention, the "blame and shame" approach described in this example does not usually have any beneficial effect on the mental health of those on either the giving or receiving end.

The employee's behaviour could not be allowed to continue. The employer felt that the behaviour would be altered if the woman was held accountable, made to accept responsibility, required to admit that her behaviour was unacceptable. The consultant was hired to accomplish this task. The humiliation that the employee endured and the distress that she and her co-workers experienced through the exercise of blaming her for her behaviour and shaming her for it, caused a severe rift in the work group and did not achieve the desired result. If the exercise had been focused on achieving practical solutions to her behaviour a more beneficial result might have been achieved.

> **Human nature responds to blame and shame tactics, unwarranted or harsh criticism, judgement or threats in predictable ways, often with withdrawal, defensiveness or counterattacks.**

Workplaces where problematic behaviour in employees is routinely met with their being called to task on performance or behavioural issues and in which they regularly have their faults and weaknesses pointed out to them and are forced to admit their shortcomings, encourage a pattern of recurrence. Seldom does this approach put an end to problems. It often results in a cycle of repeated problems without sustainable resolutions.

It is more likely that these employees will exhibit withdrawn and defensive behaviours or respond with counterattacks. All these responses have telltale signs. For example, withdrawn employees can show a lack of engagement or motivation. Defensiveness and self-justification are also common responses manifesting themselves as argumentativeness, whining or hostility, all of which is unpleasant to be around. There can be counterattacks in the form of verbal assaults on the manager or co-workers, filing of grievances and complaints, or making accusations against someone else in the workplace.

Managers, employers and supervisors who are prepared to make a sincere attempt to reach sustainable solutions value commitment over compliance. This involves helping employees to develop solutions that bring about the change necessary to have a healthy work experience and to produce or complete the tasks at hand.

While ignoring workplace problems tends to lead to even bigger problems, focusing on a solution to workplace performance or productivity issues, instead of indulging in the blame game, is likely to produce more positive results.

THE CASE OF THE OVERWHELMED SOCIAL WORKER

WHAT HAPPENED?

In the following case, Arbitrator Bendel held that even employee dishonesty and dereliction of duty can be mitigated by the fact that the employer put the individual in question under such job pressure that she made poor judgments and lost perspective.[4]

The grievor was a 24-year-old social worker. On her very first day of work, she was assigned over 30 Crown Ward cases, which would have been a heavy caseload even for an experienced social worker. The provincial standard was 22 to 24 such files per social worker. She had no prior exposure to such files. Moreover, none of the files she was assigned was in compliance with the legislation at the time, in that they lacked Plans of Care and other documents that were supposed to have been prepared.

The grievor was surprised at the volume of work she received and had to put in a lot of overtime to keep up.

At the same time as fixing deficiencies in the file documentation (which she was ordered to do), she had to respond to an unusually large number of crises affecting her wards, such as breakdowns in foster home arrangements, court appearances by the wards, etc.

The grievor eventually fell behind with her duties and engaged in some petty dishonesty involving falsification of travel claims for which she was dismissed.

In grieving the dismissal, the union claimed on her behalf that she was carrying an unusually heavy workload for such a new employee, which led to her feeling overwhelmed. During this period she had a new supervisor who exercised minimal supervision over her and did not realize the pressure on her.

---

[4]   *Children's Aid Society of Ottawa-Carleton v. O.P.S.E.U.*, 2003 CarswellOnt 9275, [2003] O.L.A.A. No. 32 (Ont. Arb. Bd.).

In addition, although the employer was not fully informed of the fact at the time, she was suffering from serious medical conditions, which led her to become depressed.

She sought professional help for her depression and was prescribed medications, from the side effects of which she became confused and forgetful.

The union claimed further that the dereliction of duty and allegations of dishonesty etc. were largely attributable to her overwork, confusion and forgetfulness, as well as to her misguided attempts to cover up her shortcomings in order to save herself from embarrassment.

The arbitrator accepted the union's claim in part, saying,

> I view the grievor's misconduct in this case as being closely related to the emotional state she was in as a result of her workload and lack of support. Although I have not been satisfied that the health concerns she relied on have been proven, the evidence as a whole tends to confirm that she was 'a total mess' (to use her phrase) in the summer and fall of 2001.

> I do not regard the lies she told the employer as evidence that she is not a person who can be trusted. Rather I view them as a product of her feeling of being overwhelmed. While this explanation does not excuse her conduct it does tend to negate the employer's argument that the employment relationship is not salvageable.

> In these circumstances I am satisfied that the discharge should be set aside. It would not be appropriate, however, to award her compensation for lost salary and benefits.

The legal reasoning in the case of the *Overwhelmed Social Worker* is sparse. It is clear, however, that the arbitrator intended the exercise of management rights be subject to the requirement that it should not, knowingly and negligently, be injurious to employee mental health as a result of excessive job demands and lack of support.

But how can employers meet this standard of care?

Suggested Strategies

Here are three possibilities, consistent with advice given so far in the two previous cases.

Ensure that Extra Effort Involves Group Participation

In most work situations, there are times where there is more work than the existing staff can accomplish in a 35-hour work week. It is not unreasonable to expect employees to pitch in and help from time to time and put in some extra effort. Going the extra mile may actually bring workers together, improve camaraderie and build pride. This occurs most often when the extra work is taken on as a team effort with all players supporting one another to accomplish a given task. Positive outcomes are much less likely when the extra effort is demanded of an employee working alone or with no support or recognition, or when these demands become the norm rather than an exception.

When assigning extra work, it is usual to choose the person you know will complete the task on time and do a good job. Problems arise when this becomes a standard procedure: one person being assigned the majority of extra work. It's not unlike a runner first to cross the finish line getting rewarded with the requirement to do an extra lap.

Rewarding your most efficient and competent workers with more work has the tendency to result in their feeling burnt out and exploited. On the other hand, other workers may see the situation differently, seeing the assignments as favouritism in that the one employee is given more of an opportunity to shine. The result is that your star employee is forced to accept more work while suffering the resentment of co-workers. When extra work is a team effort, unintended negative consequences are reduced and the extra work is not an unreasonable demand on any one person.

Prioritize for Productivity

If employees don't speak up when they are overwhelmed or unable to complete their tasks, how is an employer to know they are distressed? Employees need clear direction from their managers and supervisors that the volume of work will continue to flow at a consistent rate. However, unless employees come forward and ask for help in prioritizing, employers are often unaware of how many demands any particular employee is juggling. Unless there is proof to the contrary, the employer makes the assumption that the employees are fine. Employers and managers need to recognize that it is not always possible to be aware that employees are being overwhelmed by the volume of the work. It's essential to keep lines of communication open so that it clear to employees that there is always an opportunity to discuss the workload and that it is not the employer or manager's intention to overload any one individual.

Workplace Interventions: Accounts from the field
Analyze and Prioritize

The work team regularly complained about having too much to do and not enough time. The manager was confused because the productivity of the team was going down rather than up. To find out what was happening, the manager asked all staff to record what they did for one week in 15 minute increments. Although this request was received with much groaning that it would only add to the problem of time management, the manager said that he was unable to assess and prioritize for them if he was unaware of how their time was spent. His goal was to ensure that each person had a reasonable workload and he needed this information to do that.

The results of this exercise surprised everyone. Many workers found that they were spending an inordinate amount of time on activities such as frequent checking of email. If email checking was reduced to two or three time slots each day, it would be much more efficient and allow for full concentration on other tasks during the rest of the time. Multi-tasking was stressing workers and reducing the quality of work produced. Schedules were reorganized to create blocks of time so that one task could have exclusive attention in each block. The number of meetings had reached unreasonable levels and they were often seen as "a waste of time." The team decided to establish a rule that meetings should only be called with a clear agenda in place and with action items being recorded and distributed afterward. This helped to reduce the total number of impromptu or poorly planned meetings.

Finally, it was discovered that for years some employees were actually doing tasks that were irrelevant to their work. This had happened because procedures were still in place that required a review or recording of information that was no longer used. These tasks were simply eliminated.

Overall, this one week of painful recording of work resulted in re-evaluating priorities and as a result freed up time and improved quality of work.

- **Require employees to get help prioritizing when they cannot complete the work assigned within working hours.**

- **Priorities may be based on urgency, value to the bottom line, and/or essential duties.**

- **Establish how time is being spent by requesting that employees complete a work log.**

- **Reduce interruptions.**

- **Increase the ability to focus exclusively on one task at a time.**

- **Ensure meetings are productive and necessary.**

- **Review regular/routine tasks to assess their value.**

The Overtime Paradox

In the following example, a business in an office environment, there was a "no overtime" rule. The majority of employees were parents of young children, as was the employer. If an employee could not complete their assigned work during working hours, it was policy to have a discussion about what the options were and figure out what was to be done together.

In some cases, help was provided by co-workers who were not currently under as much pressure. In other instances, if a few hours of uninterrupted work would do the trick, the individual who had trouble getting work finished in time was given the opportunity to direct his or her full attention to the work at hand—phone calls were sent to voicemail, any meetings were cancelled or postponed. In rare circumstances the employee *would* get permission to do a few hours of overtime. However this was closely monitored so that it did not become a regular activity.

At one point it was decided that an additional employee was needed, and the team assisted in developing a job description and mentoring the individual who was hired. In the eight years this process was in place and being monitored, the organization and the individuals who worked there thrived. Helping each other out when needed created and sustained a sense of loyalty, dedication and camaraderie. The bottom line result was a three-fold increase in profit. The overtime paradox is that when people consistently work long hours, their productivity usually goes down on a consistent basis. Longer hours through overtime do not usually result in overall improvement in quality, productivity or performance.

Some employers worry that this policy will result in *everyone* coming and saying they are overloaded with work and want to do less. However this approach reduces your risk of finding out too late that an employee workload situation has become critical. An additional benefit is that when employees feel they are not isolated or overwhelmed, their focus, productivity and loyalty often increase.

Mistake Meetings

Employees who feel that they cannot share their problems or mistakes tend to hide them. Attempts to cover up what is really happening can take the form of falsifying records, neglecting to report client dissatisfaction or denying knowledge about missing or damaged property. Deceit of this type can create considerable damage to the reputation and viability of any organization. Bosses who represent themselves as people who never make mistakes and for whom nothing less than constant workplace excellence is acceptable may inadvertently invite this type of deception.

As an alternative, consider the practice of one innovative organization that has monthly "Mistake Meetings." During the meeting, the leader shares one or more mistakes that he or she had made in the past month and describes what was done to correct the situation or, if the error has not been resolved, asks for help to correct the problem. As the meeting progresses each of the team members in turn share significant mistakes they have made in the past month and follow the same pattern either describing the solutions or asking for help.

> **The message conveyed through this process is that we all make mistakes and together we will solve them; it encourages openness in workplace problem solving and reduces the damage of mistakes when they are made.**

The added bonus to the organization is that the process of sharing these experiences diminishes the probability of repeating declared errors. By helping team members solve problems together they can also avoid similar ones in the future—and sometimes this also results in unexpected innovation and creativity. The benefits of this approach serve to introduce the next chapter which focuses on work environments where it is safe to speak up about concerns for psychological safety or well-being that may impact work performance.

CHAPTER 3

The Duty to Provide a Psychologically Safe Workplace: Making it Safe to Speak Up

Many conflicts and dysfunctions in the workplace begin with the apprehension that it is not safe to speak up.

The earliest concept of psychological safety at work had at its core these shared perceptions:

- workers would not be penalized or disadvantaged for giving voice to concerns or opinions about the means, manner or methods of work in their teams or units; and

- it was safe to declare relevant facts about personal situations that were having, or might have, an impact on individual or team job performance.

This remains true today: psychological safety thrives in an atmosphere of trust that results from the freedom to voice concerns and opinions and to declare relevant facts about personal situations that may impact upon job performance. The creation of an atmosphere of trust is a key employer responsibility in the domain of psychological safety.

In the absence of basic trust, misinformation, misunderstanding, false assumptions and a climate of ill-will are likely to flourish. These are the very conditions that in turn contribute to the likelihood that someone caught up in such a vortex of mistrust will see him or herself (rightly or wrongly) as having been mentally injured.

The legal cases described in this chapter illustrate various instances in which a failure of "safe voice" led or contributed to misperceptions, misinformation, and false assumptions that spawned claims of mental injury of one kind or another.

THE CASE OF THE TROUBLED TECHNICIAN

WHAT HAPPENED?

Kimberly Bertrend filed a complaint against Golder Associates Ltd. ("Golder"), alleging discrimination in employment based on physical and mental disability, contrary to s. 13 of the B.C. Human Rights Code.[1]

Ms. Bertrend was an Environmental Technician who worked for Golder at different times and in various locations from May 2006 until she was terminated on August 28, 2007.

She worked in that capacity in Golder's Whitby, Ontario, office from May to December 2006.

After she and her boyfriend moved to British Columbia, she commenced employment at Golder's Abbotsford office on June 4, 2007, as an *Engineering* Technician, however, the office was aware that she eventually planned to transfer back to the *environmental* sector.

Because Golder had paid for Ms. Bertrend's moving allowance, there was an agreement that she would work a full 12 months, otherwise she would have to pay back the moving allowance.

Ms. Bertrend was unsatisfied with her work at the Abbotsford office and testified that it got to the point that there was virtually no work for her to do and she had little guidance.

---

[1]   *Bertrend v. Golder Associates Ltd.*, (2009), 2009 BCHRT 274, 2009 CarswellBC 2204 (B.C. Human Rights Trib.).

She was also having personal difficulties. She required hospitalization for a brief period of time, and she cried at work on two occasions while at the Abbotsford office.

She disclosed her depression to her *non-management* colleague in the Abbotsford office.

On July 9, 2007, Ms. Bertrend sent an e-mail to a Golder Human Resources employee expressing interest in switching offices. She wanted to explore a transfer to the North Vancouver office, where Golder had its largest environmental lab in the Lower Mainland. She indicated that she wanted to stay with Golder and build her career with it. She referred to the commute as being the main reason for seeking a transfer in her e-mail, but testified that the main reason was she felt unproductive in the Abbotsford office. She also sent an e-mail to her employer at the Abbotsford office, expressing her dissatisfaction with the work there and her intent to transfer.

Ms. Bertrend was transferred to the Surrey office on a temporary basis. One of the reasons the onsite manager agreed to the transfer was because Ms. Bertrend's boyfriend worked in the Surrey office and the onsite manager wanted to ensure he stayed with them. However, the onsite manager felt that Ms. Bertrend had no long-term commitment to Surrey, as she had often expressed her desire to work in the North Vancouver office.

The Surrey onsite manager scheduled a meeting with Ms. Bertrend to discuss an offer. When Ms. Bertrend arrived for the meeting, the onsite manager was on the phone with the Abbotsford employer, and they were discussing Ms. Bertrend.

Ms. Bertrend overheard the onsite manager make the following comment: "I don't think she deserves a permanent offer ... seems she doesn't want to stay here ... I'll let you know if she tears up." The onsite manager was laughing when she said this.

The tribunal inferred from the circumstances that the "tears up" comment was in reference to the times when Ms. Bertrend had previously cried in the workplace.

The Surrey offer was that Ms. Bertrend would be an hourly paid employee with no benefits and no guarantee of hours. Ms. Bertrend was unhappy with this offer. She asked for reasons and the "tears up" comment was discussed.

Ms. Bertrend then disclosed to the onsite manager that she suffered from depression. She said she did not know what to say about the offer and would get back to the onsite manager on Friday.

Ms. Bertrend then sent an e-mail to Golder's Regional Human Development Manager, detailing the meeting with the Surrey onsite manager. Later that evening, the onsite manager sent Ms. Bertrend an apologetic e-mail and within it, acknowledged Ms. Bertrend's depression and reminded her that the Employee Assistance Program was available.

Ms. Bertrend was away from work for two days, during which time she consulted with a lawyer.

She returned on August 23 for a meeting with the Surrey onsite manager and Human Development Manager to discuss her options. Later that evening, Ms. Bertrend sent the Human Development manager an e-mail saying she was not interested in being laid off, and that she was interested in negotiating an offer that would allow her to continue working in Surrey.

Ms. Bertrend was still an employee at the Abbotsford office, even though she was working temporarily in Surrey. Her employer decided that he was not willing to put further time and resources into training someone who was not interested in the work. He heard from the Surrey office that there was not going to be a position for Ms. Bertrend there. He decided to terminate, and wished to do so quickly, as Ms. Bertrend's probationary period was coming to an end.

At the time he made this decision, he was not aware that Ms. Bertrend suffered from depression.

There was a meeting scheduled for him and Ms. Bertrend on August 28 at the Abbotsford office. On the morning of August 28, Ms. Bertrend saw a doctor who advised her to take time off work. At the time, she was getting sick almost every day, not eating at all, and having panic attacks. She tried to find out where to send the medical note, but was not advised. The note said that she was unable to work for 8-12 weeks due to major depression.

Ms. Bertrend's employer decided to proceed with termination even though Ms. Bertrend was not present at the meeting. He adjusted the termination letter to reflect her absence, and couriered it to her at her home. The courier returned the letter, so he sent an e-mail to Ms. Bertrend's Golder and private e-mail addresses with the letter attached. He then re-sent the e-mails twice more to make sure she received them.

On August 29, the employer called Ms. Bertrend to verify that she received the letter. She did not acknowledge receipt, and he proceeded to terminate over the phone. He then couriered a hardcopy of the letter to Ms. Bertrend's home.

She received the letter seven times.

The tribunal found that a case of discrimination had been made and awarded damages accordingly.

WHAT COULD HAVE BEEN DONE DIFFERENTLY?

When an employer discovers that an employee is suffering from a disability, including depression, there is a duty to accommodate that employee to a reasonable degree. Using signs of depression or other mental illness as a reason for terminating or otherwise penalizing the employee can be characterized as discrimination on the grounds of mental disability contrary to the B.C. Human Rights Code, s. 13.

Depending on the circumstances, the conduct of the employer who violates this policy can be also characterized as an assault upon personal dignity and damages may be awarded accordingly, as in this case.

At no point is it acceptable to deride or otherwise make fun of a person who exhibits signs of depression.

Suggested Strategies
Demand Professionalism from Management

Engaging in hurtful gossip at the management level has no place in the workplace. An atmosphere of gossip is not conducive to professional behaviour. Management has to be held to a higher standard. The expectation is that managers and supervisors should not stoop to petty or malicious gossip and instead should be setting an example of professional conduct.

Codes of Conduct are fairly common now, but in terms of management they may not be explicit enough or tied to performance evaluation. The adage that what gets measured gets done, applies to management approaches as well. Where the approachability of a manager by employees is measured, it is much more likely to be a focus for improvement.

Approachability not only can increase efficient problem identification and resolution, it can make a difference in employee engagement and satisfaction.

In a special 2010 forum hosted by the Mental Health Commission of Canada in Vancouver, British Columbia, the interpersonal competence or emotional intelligence of those responsible for supporting, supervising or managing employees was identified by the participants as a key component in providing a psychologically safe workplace.

Simply acknowledging employees on a daily basis where possible may seem like common sense, but some managers say that they rarely see their direct reports and very seldom have one-on-one conversations.

It takes time to recognize and respond to an employee's distress, but time pressures and job demands mean that some managers focus the majority of their attention on workflow rather than on employees. This makes it impossible to identify employee distress and unlikely that it will be responded to in a timely manner. Ensuring that managers have the time to appropriately respond to employee distress is only part of the solution. Having the competence to do so is another.

> **Hiring, evaluation of and promotion to supervisory or management roles should include a consideration of interpersonal competence along with any other technical or strategic skills required.**

Use the Rule Out Rule

During the approximately ten years the Global Business & Economic Roundtable on Mental Health operated, the principle of the Rule Out Rule was popularized by Bill Wilkerson, its chair and founder. The rule requires that, in ambiguous workplace situations involving deteriorating job performance or undesirable conduct, health problems should be ruled out before starting discipline or termination proceedings.

Human Rights and other Tribunals have on occasion recognized that having a mental illness may distort the individual's view of his or her own situation. While the employee may see the current situation as the result of stressors at work or in his or her personal life, he or she may fail to recognize it as symptomatic of a health condition that requires treatment. The employer may also have failed to notice a pre-existing condition. At times like these, the Rule Out Rule is a handy guiding principle to fall back on.

Ignoring an employee's distress is not a practical option. As a default position it often leads to a worsening of the situation. When behaviours occur that are not the norm for a worker, when performance begins to change, when employees begin to exhibit distress on the job, it is prudent to examine if there is a possibility that a health condition, including mental illness, may be responsible. This route not only encourages a more compassionate approach to addressing behaviour or performance problems, it is also in line with the approach recommended by human rights law when disability triggers the duty to accommodate.

Inquiring directly of the employee about any health conditions that may be affecting his or her performance can be a first step. Initially the individual may not be very responsive to the employer's concern or choose to say it's nobody's business. Nevertheless inquiring directly can eventually lead to a solution.

Whatever the source of the employee's distress, if this is witnessed by an employer, common decency dictates a discrete inquiry about the individual's well-being.

Respond to Employee Distress

Some managers and supervisors feel that it is an invasion of privacy to comment on emotional distress, others think that it may be embarrassing to say anything. Others may feel that the emotional distress is just a ploy for sympathy or an attempt to control a situation. For some individuals, the lack of response to their distress can confirm their belief that they should not speak up, or that they are not being heard when they do speak, or their distress is not validated. They are left with feelings (often brought on by mental illnesses) that no one cares, the situation is hopeless or that they are all alone.

When mental health is a factor in performance, a caring exchange between the employer or manager and the employee provides an opportunity to share information about the various supports and resources offered by the organization or within the community, and it opens the door to a later conversation if the individual needs to seek accommodation.

By having this conversation, the employer can demonstrate that it is safe to speak up and that there will be a reasonable attempt to help the employee. An added benefit of this approach for the employer or manager is that, if documented, the conversation will provide evidence of having offered accommodation.

Had the Abbotsford employer initiated this conversation in a genuine attempt to help, it is hardly likely they would have been as cynical or flippant about the "tearing up."

The challenge for many employers is how to accommodate mental illnesses such as depression. Some feel that simply expecting less from the employee is the only option. This approach can lead to a worsening of the employee's symptoms as their sense of value and contribution is diminished. It can also lead to resentment by other employees who are required to take on the burden of the work that used to be done by their co-worker and can leave the supervisor or manager in the tough position of having to meet the same bottom line outcomes with an employee who is not productive.

An alternative is to explore options and accommodation approaches that allow the employee to maintain a reasonable contribution in spite of the disability, which is the intent of the Human Rights duty to accommodate.

THE CASE OF THE WORKER WHO KNEW SHE WAS WRONG

WHAT HAPPENED?

This case from Manitoba illustrates some of the difficulties associated with trying to accommodate employees who have mental health issues but who appear to have sufficient volition that they can be considered, at least to some degree, culpable for misconduct.[2]

In this instance, the employee's long standing mental illness appears to have had little to do with the way her work was managed and organized over the first 25 years, although she claimed that in recent months her anxiety and depression had been exacerbated by an unsympathetic supervisor. So much so, in fact, that she absented herself and was subsequently placed on unpaid medical leave.

During this period of leave, she entered her supervisor's office without authorization, rifling through his filing cabinet searching, she said, for evidence to defend herself against her supervisor's allegations of misconduct that had led to her being reprimanded for insubordination and given a one day suspension.

She had engaged in similar behaviour two years previously.

---

[2]   *Manitoba (Dept. of Family Services and Housing) v. Manitoba Government Employees' Union*, [2009] M.G.A.D. No. 12 (Werier).

This time, she was fired.

In responding to her Union's claim that her discharge was inappropriate and unjustified, the arbitrator had to decide to what extent her conduct was volitional and to what extent driven by her mental health condition, over which she had little control beyond taking her medications.

He opted for the "hybrid" approach which has been gaining in popularity in recent years, having been used with some success in cases of alcohol and drug dependence.

He found that the grievor was not fully culpable for her misconduct because of her mental state, but was sufficiently aware that her actions were wrong that some blame should adhere.

He reasoned further that the employer, although it had tried to address the grievor's admitted difficulties in performing her job over the last two years, had failed to make sufficient inquiries into her mental state.

While the grievor could have been more forthcoming in some respects, she was not to blame for the employer's failure to form a more complete picture of her condition from medical evidence that was available.

In short, there is a proactive duty on the part of employers to gather enough medical information to enable it to decide on boundaries between culpability and non-culpability regarding employee misconduct.

The remedy in this case was to reinstate the employee subject to a one month suspension, placing her on sick leave until she became eligible for her pension.

In reaching this decision, the arbitrator allowed medical evidence that became available only *after* the notice of dismissal, arguing that it spoke to the issue of accommodation and should be allowed. This illustrates that not having the medical evidence in hand does not excuse the employer from the duty to accommodate.

WHAT COULD HAVE BEEN DONE DIFFERENTLY?

Reading between the lines in this case, it is apparent that an employee's mental illness can be seen as a source of psychological distress for others within the workplace.

One person's mental illness can become another person's nightmare if the focus is entirely on how management and/or co-workers should accommodate an individual's defined illness.

This case obliquely raises the question of the extent to which an employee living with a mental illness retains sufficient capacity to appreciate the impact that he or she is having on those around them and further begs the question, to what degree does such an employee bear some responsibility for actively participating in the creation and maintenance of an equitable and psychologically safe work environment?

The following case is another example of a hybrid situation that demonstrates the law is a very blunt instrument for dealing with such matters. It often leaves all stakeholders feeling battered and bruised. How are such complex situations to be dealt with in order to avoid legal altercations?

THE CASE OF THE WORKER WHO DIDN'T DECLARE

WHAT HAPPENED?

Mr. Lane was hired by ADGA as a quality assurance analyst. His responsibilities included "mission safety critical" work, such as artillery software testing.

A few days after he commenced his employment, Mr. Lane advised his supervisor that he had bipolar disorder and required accommodation.

The accommodation that he requested included monitoring for indicators that he might be moving towards a manic episode; contacting his wife and/or doctor; and occasionally allowing him to take time off work to avert a situation where he could move from a pre-manic stage to a full-blown episode. His supervisor gave Mr. Lane no assurances, but undertook to get back to him.

As Mr. Lane became more stressed and anxious about management's response to his accommodation request, he began to exhibit pre-manic symptoms.

Although Mr. Lane's supervisor and manager were aware of his condition when they met with him a few days later, they did not address any of his needs, they did not consider putting the meeting off to get more information, and they did not obtain legal advice. Instead, they immediately terminated his employment, which triggered a severe reaction that led to full-blown mania. Mr. Lane was hospitalized for 12 days, after which he experienced severe depression due to his inability to obtain other work. His financial position deteriorated, he had to sell his house and his marriage ended.

In its decision, the Tribunal held that management terminated Mr. Lane because of his disability and perceptions related to his disability, with virtually "no investigation as to the nature of his condition or possible accommodations within the workplace."[3]

The Tribunal further found that ADGA had breached the procedural duty to accommodate, and this itself constituted a form of discrimination. The procedural duty to accommodate required *those responsible to engage in a fuller exploration of the nature of bipolar disorder... and to form*

---

[3] *Lane v. ADGA Group Consultants Inc.* (2008), 2008 CarswellOnt 4677, [2008] O.J. No. 3076, 91 O.R. (3d) 649 (Ont. Div. Ct.).

a better prognosis of the likely impact of (Mr. Lane's) condition in the workplace."

The Tribunal also rejected ADGA's argument that Mr. Lane had an obligation to disclose his disability during the hiring process. The Tribunal held that if Mr. Lane *had* revealed this information, it would have likely triggered a stereotypical reaction in most employers about his ability to do the job, leading to a decision not to hire and no opportunity to explore possible accommodations.

In awarding damages, the Tribunal wrote, "[t]his was an instance where [the employer's] lack of awareness of its responsibilities under the Code as an employer was particularly egregious. There were no workplace policies in place dealing with persons with disabilities. Moreover, senior management were singularly oblivious to those obligations...."

The Tribunal found ADGA's dismissal of Mr. Lane to be "not only precipitate and unaccompanied by any assessment of Mr. Lane's condition but also callous to the extent of its consequences in the sense that nothing was done on the day to ensure that Mr. Lane in his pre-manic condition reached his home safely and sought medical attention."

The Tribunal awarded Mr. Lane $35,000 as general damages; $10,000 for mental anguish; a further $34,278.75 in special damages, as well as pre- and post-judgement interest.

With respect to public interest remedies, the Tribunal ordered ADGA to establish a written anti-discrimination policy and retain a consultant to provide training to all employees, supervisors, and managers on the obligation of employers under the Code, with a focus on the accommodation of persons with mental health issues.

Commenting on the decision, Ontario Human Rights Chief Commissioner Barbara Hall stated, "[t]his is a precedent-setting case for mental health disability in Ontario. Employers need to realize the risks in summarily dismissing someone with conditions like bipolar disorder."

"The duty to accommodate is a reality," she added. "At the systemic[4] level, the decision clearly reinforces the necessity for employers to take all requests for accommodation seriously and process them appropriately. At the personal level, the devastating impact of the events on the life of Mr Lane would have been very different had a real effort been made to explore with him and implement creative and individualized solutions."

In upholding the decision of the Tribunal, the Divisional Court reviewed the case law in some depth and concluded that the actions of the employer were indeed reckless and exhibited a failure to anticipate the reasonably foreseeable consequences of its refusal to accommodate the mental health condition of its employee.

The Court also upheld the public interest remedies required by the Tribunal, as noted above.

WHAT COULD HAVE BEEN DONE DIFFERENTLY?

While the duty placed on the employer in this case may seem onerous, the transcript reveals that Mr. Lane had worked for another employer while suffering from the same condition and had thrived in that environment.

There, he had taken the same approach that later failed at ADGA: he warned his employer of his condition subsequent to hiring and provided a list of things to do if he started showing signs of mania. The accommodations provided by the employer took the form of re-assigning work when Lane had to be absent in the same way that one might do when an employee is sick from any other cause. Lane received excellent performance reviews in that company.

---

[4]   Hall's use of this language foreshadowed the now broader powers of the Ontario Human Rights Commission under Bill 107 with regard to systemic remedies. Bill 107, an amendment to *Ontario Human Rights Code, R.S.O. 1990, c. 19* became effective June 2008.

The public interest remedies of the Tribunal and of the Human Rights Commission are indeed of great potential significance to employers in that such remedies may take the form of intrusions into management rights.

Suggested Strategies

The essential message to employers is that they must elicit trust even on the part of *prospective* employees if they want to possess themselves of crucial information that will allow them the opportunity to plan and execute adequate accommodations. This is best done by carefully explaining at the point of hiring the policies and procedures that the employer has in place to address mental disorders should they arise. If this does not elicit declarations from prospective employees who have mental disabilities, it cannot then be said that the employer did not discharge its duties.

> **The precautionary principle suggests that the best course of action is to pre-empt legal entanglements by preparing, implementing and monitoring policies that ensure a psychologically safe workplace.**

This means that in order to elicit employee "voice" it is advisable to have conversations that indicate it will be safe to declare personal health challenges at the point of hiring rather than at some later time when such a declaration could cause employer panic and precipitous action, as in Mr. Lane's case.

Not all disabilities can be reasonably accommodated and sometimes termination is the ultimate response to the inability of an employee to perform the essential duties of the job.

Neither the tribunal nor the court said that Mr. Lane would have been confirmed in his position had attempts been made to accommodate him; it said only that a reasonable attempt to accommodate had not occurred.

It is for this reason that all employers should have a process in place that explores the possibilities *in collaboration with* the employee.

On occasion there are situations where the desire to accommodate can be carried too far by well meaning employers. In one circumstance, an obviously distraught, but compassionate manager asked how to accommodate someone who had recently started to talk about aliens taking over the workplace and tapping into the phone. The vast majority of people who suffer from mental illnesses such as depression or common anxiety-related disorders rarely experience a psychotic break from reality. But if this occurs, it is usually no more reasonable to accommodate psychosis than it is to accommodate a seizure or a heart attack while it is occurring. These situations require treatment or intervention rather than a work accommodation. Only when it is established that the condition does not present a risk of harm to self or others should workplace accommodation be attempted.

When employees are dealing with mental illness and unable to function at work, they need help in the form of treatment and support or resources. What is not reasonable or productive is to leave them to fend for themselves and struggle in the work environment with an active episode of illness. Once the illness is brought under control to the extent that the employee can function at a reasonable level, the employer should discuss ways to allow them to gradually return to work.

When someone is in medical crisis, and there is little doubt that psychosis would be considered a medical crisis, leaving them at work is hardly likely to be in their best interests. In Mr. Lane's case, if his condition was obviously unstable, then requiring him to seek help before other approaches or accommodations were discussed would be both humane and reasonable. Once he was well again and his condition was under control, a discussion about accommodation could take place. The health and safety issues and his capacity to complete essential duties could be explored. Only when this has been fully examined and quantified should any decisions about termination be entertained.

Discrimination on the basis of disability

Sometimes workplaces institute policies or procedures that have unintended consequences. If these consequences have the *effect* of discriminating against someone with a disability, benign intent or absence of intent to discriminate does not protect the employer from the censure of human rights tribunals.

Workplace Interventions: Accounts from the field

A woman who worked in a testing laboratory became ill with depression and her performance had slipped. All work at this laboratory was quantified for scientific purposes, but this quantification had the added function of tracking productivity. If productivity was reduced by 20% or more, the employee would receive a disciplinary letter that then went into their personnel file.

This laboratory worker had recently received such a letter and was concerned that her treatment for depression would not 'kick in' before she received another letter which would bring her closer to termination. The thought of losing her job created serious levels of anxiety that were only adding to her suffering.

When the woman sought advice from a mental health agency she was asked how her productivity compared to the standard. She said that there was no standard that she knew of, but that she had always been a top performer at around 50% higher productivity than most of her colleagues. In her case even a 20% drop in productivity still placed her well above the norm.

She was then asked if there were any other behaviours or problems in the workplace—coming in late, leaving early, conflict, etc. Her answer was no and the disciplinary letter actually commented on her good attitude and pointed out that her past performance had never dropped to the present level.

Could the organization she worked for be guilty of discrimination on the basis of a disability?

She was advised to return the letter back to the employer and explain that she was experiencing a disability as defined by the *Human Rights Act* and that discipline for continuing to perform at acceptable levels could be construed as discrimination.

About a week after she returned the letter she received a letter of apology from her employer. The letter was retracted and she was thanked for pointing out a process that did not take into account the unique circumstances of each individual or the possibility of disability. Her employer amended the policy and the woman was able to continue working through to her recovery from her bout of depression.

> **If the reason for reduction in productivity is directly related to depression AND the reduction still leaves performance at a reasonable standard when compared to other workers, then the discipline was not warranted.**

There is no one-size-fits-all approach to management of employee performance, although employers may think that this would make things easier. Organizations must be aware of the way in which policies, practices or procedures may impact persons with disabilities and persons who are experiencing emotional distress at work. In this situation, human rights litigation was avoided by an employer responding appropriately to an employee concern. Had the employee felt unsafe in speaking out, the results could have been much worse for the employer who had clearly discriminated on the basis of a disability.

THE CASE OF THE DILIGENT CREW PERSON

WHAT HAPPENED?

After 23 years of exemplary service with McDonald's Restaurants of Canada, Deena Datt's employment was terminated when she developed a skin condition that prevented her from washing her hands in accordance with the company's hourly hand-washing policy.[5]

Ms. Datt began working as a crew person at the McDonald's restaurant located on Marine Drive in Vancouver in 1981.

In January 2002 she developed a painful skin condition on the tips of her fingers which progressively worsened until she had to leave work on short-term disability.

She was able to return to work in April, but after two weeks her skin condition returned and she went off work again. She attempted a second return to work in January 2003, but her condition again flared up and she began receiving long-term disability benefits in February 2003.

Neither the complainant's family doctor nor two skin specialists were able to determine the cause of her dermatitis, but the condition improved with topical treatments when she was off work. Throughout her treatment, the complainant's doctors were in constant contact with the

---

[5]   *Datt v. McDonald's Restaurants of Canada Ltd.* (2007), 2007 BCHRT 324, 2007 CarswellBC 3418 (B.C. Human Rights Trib.).

disability benefits provider, and advised in a Modified Work Restriction Report in April 2003 that the complainant should be doing "less hand washing."

When the complainant subsequently met with the rehabilitation consultant, she advised that she was eager to return to work, "hopefully with a different position," and suggested duties she could perform such as hostess, salad preparation wearing gloves, and working at the drive-through counter.

She also explained that she loved her job, viewed her co-workers and customers as family and that she planned to work there until retirement. In July 2003, the complainant attempted a third return to work.

Despite expressing concerns about her limitations, she was required to perform the same duties as previously and, by August 1, was off work again.

Over the course of the following 12 months, the complainant's doctors continued to provide updated Modified Work Restriction Reports at the request of the benefit provider. The assessments variously indicated that the complainant could not do "wet work or frequent hand washing;" that she could not "currently" return to a restaurant position with McDonald's but could at some point; that her limitations "eliminated restaurant work" of any kind as a vocation; and in a report dated August 25, 2004, that the complainant could return to work in an administrative capacity or in a position that did not require "frequent hand washing, food preparation, or the wearing of plastic gloves."

Also during this time the complainant continued to meet with the rehabilitation consultant, and repeatedly expressed her desire to return to McDonald's, identifying tasks that were within her limitations. The consultant, after determining that there were no administrative positions available, advised the complainant in August 2004 that she would not be able to return to work at McDonald's.

Insisting that there were duties she *could* perform and that McDonald's should accommodate her, the complainant obtained an appointment with a human resources consultant at head office.

Although she believed the purpose of the meeting was to discuss modified duties, the complainant was advised at the meeting that her employment was being terminated and that the decision had already been finalized.

This meeting with the HR consultant on November 8, 2004, was the first time anyone at McDonald's had met with the complainant to discuss her situation.

A complaint was filed with the B.C. Human Rights Tribunal.

The Tribunal held that McDonald's breached its duty to accommodate Ms. Datt when it fired a dedicated 23-year employee who developed a skin condition that prevented her from complying with its hourly hand-washing policy.

Given that McDonald's took no steps to accommodate the complainant, and indeed did not even meet with her until the decision to terminate her employment had been made, the Tribunal awarded an additional $25,000 for loss of dignity and self-respect.

WHAT COULD HAVE BEEN DONE DIFFERENTLY?

Many employers rely solely on the advice of outside consultants and medical professionals. This case illustrates why employers need to engage in direct conversations with employees about situations related to their employment and possible solutions to work issues, even when outside sources are involved.

Well-intentioned consultants often have only part of the story. Doctors are primarily looking out for the medical needs of the individual. Benefits providers are interpreting the wording of the policy contract that an employer has negotiated and purchased. Rehabilitation consultants are looking at helping someone re-acquire ability. Even when everyone is doing their best work, they are not focused exclusively on the employer/employee relationship as a whole. They rarely understand the range of possibilities or limitations present in workplace realities, norms or objectives. It is unlikely that any of them can fully explore all the options for accommodation.

> **A prudent employer, while taking outside source recommendations into account, ensures that the final decision concerning accommodation is based, at least in part, on a conversation with the employee.**

There have been cases involving complex situations where neither the frontline supervisor nor the human resource professional could come up with a reasonable accommodation and it was the employee who ultimately provided a workable solution. Many busy workplaces have jobs that have evolved away from official job descriptions. The nature of the work may also have evolved. The employee who requires accommodation may have considered new ways of obtaining the same or even better outcomes. It is not uncommon for an employee who requires accommodation to come up with a new approach to the work that is then adopted by all workers.

Workplace Interventions: Accounts from the field
Addressing problems with work quality

There are numerous examples of how this evolutionary process can lead to new ways of doing things. An office worker who regularly missed important steps in her assigned tasks was disliked by co-workers whose own work was delayed or more complex when they had to deal with her mistakes.

Management's response was to call her in and point out her mistakes. This did not result in the improvement of performance they were seeking, but rather in a worsening of her depressive symptoms.

The worker, who wasn't concentrating well due to depression, was asked what she could do to improve this situation. After some thought, she offered to write out task lists that included a place to check off each step in the task. This helped her to avoid making mistakes of omission that would place a burden on co-workers. This was of benefit to her co-workers in a way that had been unforeseeable: they observed how useful her method was and actually adopted the use of the task lists themselves when training new hires.

When an employee is engaged in the development of a solution to their performance problems, they are often more committed to a successful outcome as well.

Misperceptions and Fear

An industrial worker's disability resulted in a perception that he was a threat to others which was absolutely false. His job required him to teach safe use of equipment by manually placing people's hands in the proper positions.

In time, his own team came to understand that he was not a threat. However it was thought that many who were required to take the safety training would remain unconvinced and would resist having him touching them. This presented quite a dilemma to his supervisor, manager and co-workers.

The individual himself bridled at the thought that people still had misperceptions about him. However he agreed that it would present an obstacle to his ability to do his job effectively. He developed a new way to demonstrate the safe use of equipment that did not involve touching

68

people, but was still compliant with the health and safety requirements related to the equipment.

No one else was able to provide a solution, least of all the outside consultant who was working on the case. This new approach ended up being adopted by everyone in the organization and the manuals were rewritten to reflect the process.

What would you like to do about that?

After interviews with management and co-workers, it was abundantly clear that a particular woman was not well-liked. The majority of people found her unreliable, taking a lot of days off and miserable when she was in. A couple of people even used the term "miserable bitch" to describe her.

She was 35-years old and a 15-year employee. When she was asked how others in the workplace perceived her, she responded, with a sigh, that she didn't know.

Although she had suffered with depression since she was an adolescent, she had never told anyone at work.

She realized that on a bad day, she did not even look at people, she often wouldn't answer them and sometimes she would just grunt and turn away. "I feel awful, I look awful, and I guess everyone probably thinks I'm a miserable bitch," she concluded. She was asked, "What would you like to do about that?" There was no agreement or disagreement with her conclusion, only a question about how she would like to handle the perceived reaction of other employees.

She said that she would never be Little Mary Sunshine, but that even on a bad day she would like to be able to smile and make eye contact and take an attitude of professional service. The employee decided to commit to smiling on days when she was clinically depressed. No one should have to smile on a bad day and no employer could require this of an employee but she had come to the realization "I can control how people respond to me when I'm not well. I want to have that control."

About six months after this consultation, the employee wrote a letter saying that she had a new lease on life. Although she would probably always live with depression, she now understood how to make it less tragic by helping others be supportive rather than hostile towards her.

THE CASE OF THE EXPERTS WHO COULDN'T AGREE

WHAT HAPPENED?

This is a case of a man who suffered from Chronic Fatigue Syndrome and who ran afoul of a medical and judicial process that became part of his problem rather than part of the solution.[6]

In this instance, the varying opinions of the legal and medical communities throughout the history of this case are part of the story— they are an example of how amazingly different views can be taken of the same recorded facts.

Kevin Keays had worked for Honda Canada Inc. for 11 years when he was diagnosed with Chronic Fatigue Syndrome in 1997.

He stopped working and received disability benefits until 1998, when Honda's insurer discontinued his benefits. At this point, Mr. Keays returned to work but was placed on a disability program that allowed employee absences so long as a doctor's note confirmed that the absences were related to the employee's disability.

---

[6] *Keays v. Honda Canada Inc.* (2008), 2008 SCC 39, 2008 CarswellOnt 3743, 2008 Car-swellOnt 3744 (S.C.C.).

Honda became concerned (some legal opinions placed the employer's attitude closer to "suspicious") about the frequency of Mr. Keays' absences and asked him to meet with Dr. Brennan, an occupational medical specialist in their own employ.

On advice of counsel, Mr. Keays refused to meet with Dr. Brennan without an explanation of the meeting's purpose and methodology. In March, 2000, Honda informed Mr. Keays that it supported his full return to work, but that his employment would be terminated if he refused to meet with Dr. Brennan. When Mr. Keays again refused to meet with Dr. Brennan, Honda terminated his employment.

Mr. Keays sued Honda for wrongful dismissal. The trial judge found that the plaintiff was entitled to a notice period of 15 months, and that because the employer had committed acts of discrimination and harassment against Keays, the notice period should be increased to 24 months to reflect the manner of dismissal. The trial judge also awarded punitive damages against the employer in the amount of $500,000, a costs premium, and costs on a substantial indemnity scale.

On appeal, the Court of Appeal for Ontario upheld the trial judge's decision, but reduced the punitive damages award to $100,000, as well as the costs premium.

Honda appealed this decision to the Supreme Court of Canada.

The majority of the Supreme Court held that Mr. Keays was wrongfully dismissed and the regular award of damages for 15 months notice should be maintained. But aggravated damages should not have been awarded in this case, as Honda's conduct in dismissing Keays was not in their view an egregious display of bad faith. According to the majority, there was no evidence that Mr. Keays' disability subsequent to termination was caused by the manner of termination.

Similarly, punitive damages should not have been awarded, as the facts of the case did not demonstrate acts so malicious and outrageous that they warranted punishment on their own. According to the Supreme Court, *both* lower courts erred in finding that Honda's discriminatory conduct amounted to an "independent actionable wrong" for the purpose of awarding punitive damages.

Two judges of the Supreme Court dissented in part: Justices LeBel and Fish held that the award for additional damages for the manner of dismissal *should* stand, stating that there *was* a sufficient basis for the findings of bad faith and discrimination in the manner in which Mr. Keays was terminated. They, however, agreed with the majority opinion that punitive damages should be set aside, as should the costs premium.

The judicial disagreement at the Supreme Court level in *Honda* is significant, with two judges interpreting the facts of the case in a manner different from the other seven.

The decisions and disagreements within the case are mostly about interpretations of *factual* evidence. They are not about the law except in some relatively small areas that are still in ferment.

The trial judge heard 30 days of factual testimony. It is normal for courts of appeal to defer to lower courts with regard to interpretation of facts, as noted by Justice LeBel.

There are unresolved and ambiguous issues about the relationship between employers, their insurers and their "medical experts."

The dissent contains some blunt talk about the role of company doctors and their suspect capacity as "independent medical experts."

Should insurance company decisions about employee benefits be seen as independent from those of the employer as portrayed in this case?

There are some underlying issues that get some fleeting discussion but are never quite surfaced as influencing the opinions of the court. For example: is Chronic Fatigue Syndrome a real disorder? Are "sufferers" really malingerers?

WHAT COULD HAVE BEEN DONE DIFFERENTLY?

In a situation where an employee is repeatedly expressing a need to take time off, particularly if this involves weeks or months rather than isolated days, it is reasonable for the employer to require evidence that this is medically necessary and compensable under the duty to accommodate. So much of the problem in the Honda situation, and others like it, is the intention and motivation that drives the declared need for evidence.

If there is an accepted standard of fairness towards all workers and the cost of being fair is considered a justifiable expense to the organization, then the worker will be approached with fairness.

If the intention to collect evidence is motivated by mistrust, the worker will be approached accordingly.

Malpractice Research

In his book, *Blink*,[7] Malcolm Gladwell reported a study by Wendy Levinson and others who had tried to discover if it was possible to have advance warning of which physicians would be more likely to be exposed to malpractice lawsuits.

The author concluded that it was not the quality or degree of detail in the information provided by the physician, nor was it a matter of poor medical practice. Gladwell argues that the statistical correlations indicated that it was *the way physicians spoke* to their patient that was most closely correlated with their exposure to lawsuits.

---

[7] Malcolm Gladwell, *Blink: the power of thinking without thinking* (New York: Little, Brown and Co. 2005).

Those who were less likely to be sued *talked* to patients, helping them understand the process, invited questions and discussion, and *engaged in active listening* that really focused on the patient's concerns. Those who were less likely to be sued were also far more likely to express a sense of humour and laugh with patients.

The results of this research, done with medical doctors, may have implications for the workplace. It is worthwhile considering that employees who feel heard and respected, even in difficult circumstances, respond to their managers and supervisors in kind and may be less inclined to feel that they are unfairly treated or to sue.

Common courtesy and respect for others may not be natural attributes for all managers or supervisors but they can be skills that are required as part of a professional demeanour that employers can demand of their managers if for no other reason than to reduce exposure to lawsuits.

Workplace Interventions: Accounts from the field
Accepting Change

Sometimes having a professional demeanour requires a restriction to what some employees may feel is their freedom of speech or "voice" especially if their conduct is of long standing and rooted in tradition.

Norms change. Perceptions of what is acceptable change. Sometimes conduct that was commonplace becomes unacceptable.

An all-male emergency services work environment had an in-house harassment complaint filed against it that involved allegations of name-calling. The respondents stated that this was not a case of name-calling but just the use of a nickname given in the spirit of fun. The decision was made by management to prohibit the use of nicknames.

Many of the workers were outraged by this so-called "infringement on freedom of speech" and refused to comply. They argued that it was a valued tradition to bestow a nickname on all new hires and that this was part of the camaraderie that was so important to those facing life and death situations.

Eventually, a human rights lawyer was brought in to explain to the group that anyone who continued to engage in this behaviour would face discipline and possibly even termination. The lawyer attempted to explain that what seems like good natured teasing by some, can and had been seen as harassment by others. Leaders in particular, were strongly cautioned to comply.

Most of the emergency responders were not convinced but realized that they risked losing their jobs if they continued. The name calling stopped and about a year later, one of the "traditionalists" commented that it did seem a more peaceful and content work environment after all.

In this example, the request for change did come from an employee, but in order to enact the change, the employer had to resort to threatening discipline or job loss. When human rights issues are at play, compliance is not negotiable. The fact that there was eventual recognition of the long term improvement in the work environment can be used as an example when your necessary policy changes are met with resistance.

CHAPTER 4

The Duty to Provide a Psychologically Safe Workplace:
Monitoring and Responding to Identified Risks

A commitment to provide a psychologically safe workplace includes a responsibility to identify patterns of conduct that may present risks to the mental health of employees who are exposed to them. The employer also has the added responsibility to amend these risky behaviours.

This responsibility—also referred to as "assess and address"—can be discharged in a number of ways and these will be discussed in the analyses of some of the more telling cases on this point.

There is a common feature to these cases. All the workplaces involved in these situations where transgressions took place suffered from *systemic* problems that had been ignored or simply not identified.

Such systemic problems are characteristic of the so-called *poisoned environment*. This is a term often used to describe a workplace in which there is a persistent and repetitious pattern of abusive conduct that develops over time and is ignored and allowed to continue, and/or is supported by the employer. No adequate steps are taken to correct the situation, so that eventually destructive behaviour patterns become part of the culture of the workplace.

Abusive conduct includes physical or mental mistreatment. It includes the improper or inappropriate use of power as well as behavior towards others that is unreasonable. Chronic inattention to relentless work demands, ever increasing requirements to exert greater effort and the disregard of the impact these are having on the mental health of employees can also be examples of abusive conduct.

The employer's duty to monitor and respond to identified risks to employee mental health therefore includes the requirement to identify and amend poisoned environments and abusive conduct.

Considering psychological safety throughout the employment relationship

The potential to affect psychological safety exists at all stages of the employment relationship. The employer's task is therefore to ask questions and consider approaches that are relevant to the provision of a psychologically safe workplace at all these stages.

a) Organizational Structure

Is there a stated commitment from senior leadership to provide a psychologically safe and mentally healthy workplace? Does the organization have effective two-way internal communication channels that are used on a consistent basis? Are the vision and objectives of senior leadership shared with all employees? Do employees understand how their work contributes to the overall objectives? Is leadership recognized and assessed for its ability to provide a psychologically safe work environment?

b) Job Design

Do job designs take into account a balance between effort and reward as well as demand and control? Are psychological demands—dealing with isolation, deadline pressures, high rates of change, social interactions, or exposure to trauma—considered and mitigated when designing jobs?

c) Recruiting, Hiring or Promoting

Are candidates made aware of the psychological, interpersonal demands of the job for which they are applying? Is the process used for hiring transparent and fair for all? Do you recruit or hire into positions of management only those whose skills in people management are appropriate?

d) Orientation and Training

Are employees given sufficient orientation to the culture of the organization, the resources available for those who may need them, the expectations in terms of social interactions, as well as to the tasks performed? Are employees that are new to a department or role integrated successfully with existing staff? Does training prepare employees adequately to complete their tasks effectively and is it provided on an ongoing basis to refresh the skills of longer term employees?

e) Performance Management and Discipline

Are job expectations clear and fair for everyone? Are employees supported in such a way that each is enabled to provide their best contribution to the team? Are the methods of measurement of success known and applied consistently? Are performance issues and concerns identified and resolved in a timely manner? Are employees required to take an active role in developing solutions for their own performance problems?

f) Intervention and Crisis Response

Are the policies clear about responding in times of crisis to issues of violence, harassment, natural disaster, addiction, or psychotic break and were they developed with input from all stakeholders? Is consideration given to the effect that workers with performance or behaviourial problems have on co-workers or supervisors? Are conflicts resolved effectively and with respect for all involved?

g) Accommodation and Return to Work

Is there a process that takes into account the psychological safety of those who are experiencing mental health issues at work, while off work or when returning to work, regardless of the stated cause of injury or illness? Do the processes around accommodation and return to work ensure individuals are treated with respect and that they are an active part of developing the solutions that will allow them to stay productive?

h) Redeployment and Termination

Is consideration given to the psychological safety of the individual whose role is to inform employees about re-deployment, termination, and related matters?

Do the processes embed safeguards for all stakeholders into these processes?

Are terminations and redeployments carried out according to current legal standards calling for the strict avoidance of intimidation, cruelty and humiliation?

There are other stages in employment and other questions to ask. The categories above are intended to get the conversation started. The goal is that psychological safety becomes an approach embedded in all facets of human resources and organizational design rather than an add-on policy or program.

Sometimes, psychologically unsafe, poisoned environments do not encompass the entire workplace but are micro-ecologies within larger and otherwise safe and healthy environments. However, they present a dangerous threat to employee mental health wherever they are found and no workplace can be psychologically safe while these micro-ecologies go unidentified and unchecked.

The three cases reported below raise systemic issues and commentary follows after all three are presented.

THE CASE OF THE QUICK-TEMPERED SUPERVISOR

WHAT HAPPENED?

Marta Piresferreira, a woman of Brazilian extraction, was in her mid-60s at the time of the incident that forms the focal point of this case. She worked as an account representative for Bell Mobility from 1997 to 2005 during which time she received mostly excellent performance reviews. She was a well-liked and gregarious person who became a shadow of her former self as a result, at least in part, of events that occurred in her workplace.[1]

Her supervisor during this period, Richard Ayotte, was described as a rough and ready fellow, quick to anger and prone to foul language. Ms. Piresferreira was originally the sole female member of a six-person team. She was accustomed to her supervisor's style, but never became comfortable with it. In addition, she was living in a lesbian relationship and was routinely exposed to pejorative comments about gays from her co-workers and supervisor. Indeed, all the evidence points to a poisoned environment as it might be seen from a human rights perspective.

During this period (2001) a female team coordinator was appointed who developed what the Court called an almost visceral dislike for Ms. Piresferreira. This same person was very critical of her during the trial. The team coordinator's claim was that she could "handle" Mr. Ayotte, unlike Ms. Piresferreira who withered under his abusive manner. This

---

[1] *Piresferreira v. Ayotte* (2008), 2008 CarswellOnt 7733, 72 C.C.E.L. (3d) 23 (Ont. S.C.J.) and reasons for costs order reported at *Piresferreira v. Ayotte*, (2009), 2009 CarswellOnt 3347, 74 C.C.E.L. (3d) 303 (Ont. S.C.J.); reversed *Piresferreira v. Ayotte*, (2010), 2010 ONCA 384, 2010 CarswellOnt 3551; leave to appeal refused *Piresferreira v. Ayotte*, 2011 CarswellOnt 201, 2011 CarswellOnt 202 (January 20, 2011), Doc. 33811 (S.C.C.).

person appears to have contributed to the toxic environment in which Ms. Piresferreira was working every day.

To give a flavour of the differences in plaintiff and defendant perspectives, the following extract from the finding of fact in the initial trial are reproduced below. This extract concerns how meetings were conducted within the team:

> Ayotte described the meetings as being collegial gatherings where everyone could provide his or her input. The account managers, who testified, including Piresferreira, described the team meetings in less neutral terms. Ayotte used some of those meetings to berate the team if there were problems or if targets were not being met. It was not uncommon for him to yell and swear at the group and bang his fist on the table to make a point. Ayotte described Piresferreira as being quite passive at the team meetings and as not contributing many independent ideas or suggestions. Piresferreira described herself as contributing to the meetings when she could, but at times feeling sidelined.

There is evidence, too, that Ms. Piresferreira and Mr. Ayotte began to hold different views concerning her performance and whether it needed to be improved and in what areas. Indeed in 2004, her performance did fall below expectations, but the Court found that this was for market reasons largely outside her control. It appears, too, that during this period Ms. Piresferreira was resistant to Ayotte's suggestions concerning how she might improve her performance and his response was to become progressively abusive. Ms. Piresferreira, however, could herself be rather volatile and emotional at times according to the testimony of some of her co-workers:

> Ayotte acknowledged that he had never given much thought as to whether the way he was interacting with his account managers, such as Piresferreira, might not be good for them or for the work environment. Under cross-examination, Ayotte agreed that his style could be

intimidating, it did not provide good role modeling to other employees, and it did not encourage other employees to handle themselves in a calm and professional fashion. Ayotte acknowledged that he could have handled himself differently; nevertheless, since in his mind his yelling and swearing was not an every day event, he did not believe that he was contributing to a hostile work environment. In his mind, his aggressive style was effective, and that was what counted.

In spite of these adverse dynamics in the work team, by early 2005, the Court found that Ms. Piresferreira had brought her performance back to a much higher standard and in some areas exceeded the performance norms of the team.

Later in 2005, events took a turn for the worse, culminating in an incident during which Mr. Ayotte physically shoved and pushed Ms. Piresferreira after lambasting her with more than usually humiliating and wounding comments.

As a consequence of this event and those leading up to it, which included a series of harsh and relentless criticisms, Ms. Piresferreira went off on sick leave, never to return save for a brief interlude during which she approached her supervisor with a view to soliciting an apology and was rebuffed.

During the weeks following the event, the employer issued a written reprimand to Mr. Ayotte (that the Court considered insufficient under the circumstances) requiring that he attend counselling sessions and that he issue an apology to Ms. Piresferreira. In fact, he had been referred to counselling on a previous occasion in the form of two four-hour courses on "effective communication at work" and "resolving conflict: the art of handling interpersonal tension," yet in this instance the EAP counsellor decided that he was in no further need of intervention even though Mr. Ayotte's own supervisor requested a follow-up. Apparently the counsellor took everything Mr. Ayotte said at face value.

Indeed, neither Mr. Ayotte's own supervisor nor the HR department ever undertook an independent review of the facts of this case, a fact that attracted censure from the court that first heard the case.

At one point the employer represented to Ms. Piresferreira that Mr. Ayotte had been transferred elsewhere in the company and she would no longer have to be under his supervision. This turned out to be entirely false.

Ms. Piresferreira's lawyers advised her to refuse to return to work since it was a poisoned environment. Bell Mobility responded by indicating that it considered Ms. Piresferreira to have resigned. Shortly after that, Ms. Piresferreira instituted legal action against Mr. Ayotte and the company.

The Court accepted expert evidence that Ms. Piresferreira was seriously psychologically harmed by this series of events (including the employer's weak response and later deception), and determined that the torts of battery and of intentional and negligent infliction of mental suffering had been proven. The Court accepted that she had plunged into a major episode of depression and anxiety consequent to the events complained of. Although complicated by other physical conditions from which she was suffering, her mental state was compared by one expert witness to that associated with post-traumatic stress disorder.

However, the Court of Appeal for Ontario has overturned the finding of negligent and intentional infliction of mental suffering, allowing only the battery claim and substituting a finding of constructive dismissal. The amount of damages as a result is considerably reduced since the future lost wages component of the lower court's award was rejected by the Court of Appeal and an amount only for time in lieu of reasonable notice awarded. Nevertheless, a premium was added for the manner of dismissal that was almost the same as the award given by the lower court for injury to the plaintiff's mental health.

Consider how this series of events—however it may be characterized by the law—could have been interrupted to avoid harm to the plaintiff and to avoid harm to the company that inevitably results from litigation of this kind. Regardless of who "won" this case in the end, the stress, disruption and inefficiencies resulting from the conflict and legal process remain.

THE CASE OF THE BOSS WHO PICKED WINGS OFF FLIES

WHAT HAPPENED?

Vito Stina was a mechanical service worker and back-up inspector for TTC buses. For a number of years his supervisor, Frank Zuccaro, humiliated, intimidated and marginalized him.

Among other things, Mr. Zuccaro tried to discipline Mr.Stina when it was not justified, made unwarranted complaints about his work, yelled at him and made threatening remarks. Mr. Stina was treated differently from other employees as, for example, when Mr. Zuccaro publicly ordered him back to work when others were not so ordered, restricted his telephone use but not that of others, and placed job demands and expectations upon him that were not placed upon others.

In addition, it was shown that Mr. Stina had been inadequately trained and consistently denied the opportunity to receive training for his position.

No concrete actions were taken when Mr. Stina reported the problem to the shop steward and the superintendent's office.

When he attempted to deal with the matter through the TTC's Human Rights department, he was "stonewalled" and told that there were insufficient grounds for his complaint.

Mr. Stina then went on sick leave due to anxiety and depression disorder and underwent psychiatric treatment.[2] His disorder was characterized by low energy, poor communications, tearfulness, negative self-image and poor sleep patterns.

In the end, his union took up his cause and the case went to arbitration. In arbitration, the supervisor was held liable; the employer (the TTC) was also held responsible for not having done anything to rectify the situation and for being callously indifferent to an obvious problem.

The TTC was told to make sure that the supervisor and the employee never came into contact and that if there was a danger of that, the supervisor should be the one to be moved.

Arbitrator Shime's award in this case was based on:

1. importing a term into the collective agreement to the effect that the employer has a legal duty to ensure the safety of employees and that this duty includes psychological safety. [in effect this is simply importing the Common Law duty to provide a safe system of work into the general law of collective bargaining, but Arbitrator Shime did not say so];

2. importing of the statutory duty of care from the *Occupational Health and Safety Act*, s. 25(2) to include avoidance of dealings with employees that would jeopardize their psychological safety.

---

[2] *Toronto Transit Commission v. A.T.U.* (2004), 2004 CarswellOnt 5165, [2004] O.L.A.A. No. 565, 132 L.A.C. (4th) 225 (Ont. Arb. Bd.).

These combined duties require a high standard of conduct. In Arbitrator Shime's definition, abuse includes "physical or mental maltreatment and the improper use of power. It also includes departure from reasonable conduct."

> Harassment includes words, gestures and actions which tend to annoy, harm, abuse, torment, pester, persecute, bother and embarrass another person, as well as subjecting someone to vexatious attacks, questions, demands and other unpleasantness. A single act which has a harmful effect may also constitute harassment.

In this case the employer and supervisor were held jointly and severally liable for the impact of abuse and harassment.

THE CASE OF THE WOMAN WHO DIDN'T FIT IN

WHAT HAPPENED?

In 1988, after completing three years of university, Nancy Sulz joined the RCMP in British Columbia. Shortly thereafter, she was posted to the detachment in Merritt, B.C., which consisted of 20 members, as a general duty police officer.

The head of this detachment has the rank of staff sergeant and is primarily responsible for administration, while two corporals supervise the day-to-day activities of the other members.

When the respondent joined the Merritt detachment, the commander was Staff Sergeant Stewart. He was succeeded by a temporary commanding officer, Ken Porter.

Under the supervision of both of these officers, the respondent received excellent evaluations. She was content with her progress and planned on a lengthy career with the RCMP.

In the early part of 1994, Smith became the Merritt detachment commander. At this time, the two corporals responsible for day-to-day activities were Corporals Taylor and Angell.

The respondent was married in May 1991, and her first child was born on April 16, 1993. Following maternity leave she returned to full duty in late October 1993.

In late May or early April of 1994, the respondent learned that she was unexpectedly pregnant with her second child. She continued with her regular duties until July 1994, at which point she was placed on light office duties.

On October 26, 1994, she went on medical leave because of complications with her pregnancy. Following the birth of her second child on December 12, 1994, the respondent took six months maternity leave and returned to work on June 15, 1995.

The difficulties began when the respondent was placed on light office duties. From the time when she was assigned to these duties to the time when she returned from maternity leave, the respondent was involved in at least three incidents with Smith. The first incident involved the completion of an administrative assignment, the second involved an alleged breach of RCMP policy by travelling to the USA on a shopping trip without obtaining permission, and the third incident involved her completion of forms transferring her from medical leave to maternity leave.

While on maternity leave, Ms. Sulz began to hear rumours that Smith and Angell had made numerous derogatory remarks about her in the presence of other detachment staff members. According to Ms. Sulz, the derogatory comments continued even after she returned to work. As a consequence, the respondent believed she was losing the trust of her fellow officers. These remarks related to Ms. Sulz's ability to do her job and indeed to her suitability to do it.

On June 16, 1995, Ms. Sulz contacted her divisional representative, Staff Sergeant Humphries, and provided him with a written description of these events. Following a discussion with Staff Sergeant Humphries, Ms. Sulz decided it was best to deal with the matter informally. She wanted to resolve the issue so that she could continue her career with the RCMP. Staff Sergeant Humphries viewed the matter as a serious one, and arranged to meet with Smith and Angell.

During this time, Nancy Sulz's physical and mental health deteriorated badly. She was 20 pounds underweight, unable to sleep properly and was often on the verge of tears. On June 27, 1995, she met with her family doctor who advised her to go on sick leave. On the same day, she received a telephone call from an inspector involved in the meeting with Smith and Angell, who advised her that the matter had been resolved, and she need not worry. Nonetheless, the next day she was told to stay away from the detachment because Smith was in an irate state of mind. She decided to take sick leave.

In July 1995, Ms. Sulz consulted with Dr. Carmichael, a psychologist under contract with the RCMP. He suggested that she should return to work on a part-time basis. She decided to return full-time because she wanted to try to normalize her work situation. However, the feelings of ostracism continued, and Smith avoided contact with her. The respondent also believed that her relationships with Taylor and Angell had deteriorated. In particular, the respondent and Taylor were involved in multiple disputes relating to her conduct in investigations.

On February 4, 1996, Dr. Carmichael diagnosed the respondent as having a major depressive disorder. He prescribed anti-depressants. The doctor advised her to take sick leave, and he called the detachment directly to notify her superiors that she was on sick leave. Smith telephoned Dr. Carmichael, and questioned the diagnosis. He also suggested that Dr. Carmichael may have been manipulated by the respondent.

Following the diagnosis of depression, the respondent underwent a pregnancy test that is routinely ordered before anti-depressant drugs are taken. She was surprised to learn that, despite her husband's vasectomy, she was pregnant for the third time. Because of this pregnancy, she was not able to take the anti-depressant medications. She remained under the care of Dr. Carmichael. While pregnant, the respondent remained on sick leave. In September 1996, after the birth of her third child, she went on maternity leave for six months, after which she returned to sick leave.

Thus, the respondent was on active duty with the RCMP from 1989 to April 1993, October 1993 to October 1994, and from July 1995 to January 1996. The respondent did not return to active duty after January 1996.

In May 1997, the RCMP sent the respondent to Kelowna to be examined by Dr. Semrau, a psychiatrist. He corroborated the opinions and diagnoses of Dr. Carmichael.

Following the examination, the new divisional representative, Staff Sergeant Howarth, investigated the matter and reported some concern about the conduct and history of Smith.

Staff Sergeant Howarth's report led to a formal investigation which was conducted in late 1997 and early 1998. The internal investigation culminated in a finding that discrimination had been substantiated, but that disciplinary measures could not be taken because in the meantime Smith had retired. The respondent was notified of the conclusion of the investigation in September 1998. Smith retired in April 1998.

While the formal investigation was ongoing, Ms. Sulz commenced proceedings by filing a writ of summons on July 3, 1997. She did not file a statement of claim until April 2001.

Nancy Sulz remained on sick leave until March 8, 2000, when she agreed to a medical discharge from the RCMP. She received full salary up to the date of her discharge. Upon discharge, the respondent was paid a disability pension reflecting 100% disability under s. 32 of the *Royal Canadian Mounted Police Superannuation Act*.

At the time of trial, the respondent continued to suffer from depression and remained unable to cope with any form of regular employment.

The trial judge found that Smith had committed the tort of negligently inflicting mental suffering on the respondent. Smith's harassing conduct, including "angry outbursts" and "intemperate, and at times, unreasonable behaviour" caused "serious emotional problems" and created "the troubled work environment that the plaintiff experienced."

The trial judge found that "the harassment which she experienced in 1994 and 1995 was the proximate cause of her depression, which in turn, ended her career in the RCMP." He assessed damages as follows:

General damages	$125,000
Past wage loss	225,000
Future wage loss	600,000
Total	$950,000

The Court of Appeal for B.C. basically upheld the findings and decision of the lower court.[3]

---

[3] *Sulz v. Canada (Attorney General)* (2006), 2006 BCSC 99, 2006 CarswellBC 141, [2006] B.C.J. No. 121, 54 B.C.L.R. (4th) 328, 37 C.C.L.T. (3d) 271 (B.C. S.C.), affirmed by *Sulz v. Canada (Attorney General)* (2006), 2006 BCCA 582, 2006 CarswellBC 3137, [2006] B.C.J. No. 3262, 43 C.C.L.T. (3d) 187, 60 B.C.L.R. (4th) 43 (B.C. C.A.).

WHAT COULD HAVE BEEN DONE DIFFERENTLY?

The employer in *The Case of the Quick Tempered Supervisor* knew that bad things were happening and took some steps to address them by sending the manager on training courses. However, the most expensive or most extensive training sessions in the world have little use if managers do not incorporate what they have learned and if employers fail to follow up with their managers to see how they are using their newly acquired skills in the workplace.

If the employer in this case had met with the manager and asked what the main learning points were from the course he had taken and how he was going to implement them, a basis for measuring success on how well these points had been implemented could have been established and could have been incorporated into future performance reviews. Had the employer followed through, the odds of real change occurring would have been raised considerably.

The previous three cases are primarily about the failure of employers to monitor and address risks to employee mental health embedded in the way work is managed and supervised. According to the courts and tribunal hearing the three cases, these risks could and should have been spotted by reasonably vigilant employers.

Suggested Strategies

How can employers manage this risk and discharge their responsibility? A comprehensive approach would include prevention and preparation through having the right people in the right jobs, regular assessment that allows you to stay alert to potential issues, effectively addressing issues as they arise and involving the workforce in the process.

> 1. **Prevent: Hire and promote managers and supervisors with interpersonal competence.**
> 2. **Assess: Be alert to potential issues.**
> 3. **Address: Resolve issues promptly and effectively.**
> 4. **Engage: Involve employees in developing solutions and preventing problems.**

Hire and promote managers and supervisors with interpersonal competence

In some cases, poisoned work environments are the result of system-wide, problematic interactions among people.

One important approach to prevention is to have qualified people in place to manage staff. While many individuals have excellent strategic, technical or analytical skills, this does not automatically qualify them to manage people.

The art of managing people requires a significant degree of interpersonal competence. Interpersonal competence equips a manager or supervisor with the ability to recognize and respond to the personalities, behaviours, interactions, social skills and communication styles of a diverse group of direct reports—and to do all this in a way that brings out the best in terms of productivity and potential in each person including him or herself. This is a tall order.

Separating the responsibility of strategy management from the responsibility for managing personnel may be a good option for large organizations. Those with the highest levels of interpersonal competence and leadership qualities can focus on managing and motivating employees to implement strategies and objectives developed by others whose strengths rest in those areas. Although both engage and communicate with staff, the responsibility for day-to-day interactions and the resolution of issues among co-workers rests with managers who possess the appropriate skill sets.

In smaller organizations, it may be impractical for two positions to exist at this level of management. Under those circumstances, it may be worthwhile to establish minimum interpersonal competence criteria for recruiting or promoting to management positions and to include this with the other requirements.

Employers are usually very astute at selecting and promoting employees on their technical or job specific expertise. However, the employer who wants to find a good manager with sufficient interpersonal competence looks for other indicators in the past performance of each candidate.

If the candidate has *not* had managerial or supervisory experience, the employer would primarily investigate the candidate's ability to relate or engage effectively and positively with other employees.

If the candidate *does* possess previous managerial or supervisory experience, the employer would investigate further indications of interpersonal competence. Does the candidate have the ability to recognize and mediate conflict or complaints among employees? Can he or she motivate his or her employees? What is the absenteeism rate in his or her work team? These questions and others tied to performance management, including grievances, transfers and turnover, are all clues to a potential manager's interpersonal competence.

The employer who follows these procedures as a part of a normal routine is in possession of key information that will help place appropriate managers and supervisors in positions of authority.

Even the most competent manager will run into situations that are challenging. Ensuring that they have access to just-in-time support and on-going training to deal with complex issues is good practice. Moreover, it helps to prevent mental injury to those charged with protecting the psychological safety of others in the workplace.

Be alert to potential issues

Maintaining a mentally healthy climate in the workplace requires that threats to mental health be monitored on a regular basis.

In small workplaces, being alert and checking out the expressions and behaviour of workers each day may be enough. Signs of conflict and stress can often be deduced from body language, tone of voice and styles of interaction.

Challenges to workplace mental health can be harder to discern in larger workplaces or in ones that involve satellite or remote locations of workers. There are a number of ways work environments of this size and type can proactively monitor their potential for "poisonous workplace syndrome." They range from the very informal to the highly formal. For instance, one approach to measuring risks to psychological safety, *Guarding Minds at Work,* is featured in the following chapter. It has advice on assessing and abating psychosocial risk in the workplace and was the result of a review of research and literature on workplace mental health and psychological safety. It is freely available online at: <www.guardingmindsatwork.ca>. Both formal and informal assessment methods are described in this resource, which describes both audit and survey methods.

But whether an employer chooses to conduct a psychological safety "audit" that allows senior leaders to review relevant data and statistics and consider improvements, or chooses one of two types of employee surveys to establish areas for intervention, the key imperative is: be proactive!

Many demands compete for the employer's attention and time. Strategy, planning and execution of business objectives often not only take priority, but may crowd out other concerns including health, safety or organizational culture.

Kevin Warren, CEO of Xerox Canada, is quoted as saying "culture eats strategy for breakfast." Even the best strategies and the most comprehensive plans can fail if the culture of a workplace is so poisoned that it negatively impacts the productivity and wellness of employees. The generic elements of a process to transform the culture of a workplace from the team level up are described in the next chapter.

Mediation: Resolve issues promptly and effectively

Employers often face a dilemma. Some minor spats resolve themselves in a short time without intervention: in fact, focusing attention on them can make a temporarily bad situation worse. So, when is intervention necessary? What should the nature of that intervention be? What is the prudent course of action?

Mediation is a commonly used tool in situations of conflict. Unfortunately, unskilled mediation can all too often result in there being winners and losers, with only one party, or sometimes neither party, feeling that it was a success. There are clear drawbacks to this approach. Sometimes, when one party is in a position of power over another, standard mediation can result in the person with less power agreeing to a resolution that is offered by the mediator in order to keep his or her job. Additionally, persons with stronger personalities can end up dominating the process.

When mediation ends with *both* parties feeling that they have lost, the outcome can be little more than repressed anger and restrained behaviours. This most often happens when each person is forced to accept blame for their actions, even when they feel they were justified in their behaviour. This can result in two people who feel unfairly judged and unreasonably required to engage in insincere apologies.

Sometimes the most successful mediation occurs when the resolution process focuses on solutions rather than on problems and both parties can save face and maintain their dignity. By emphasizing desirable future behaviours and outcomes and avoiding an unnecessary preoccupation with blame and failure, both people together can determine what they need to do to move forward beyond the presenting problem that brought them to mediation.

Workplace Interventions: Accounts from the field

A worker who was struggling with depression asked to be moved to another manager because he hated the one he had. As this was impossible, there was a discussion on what changes to the manager's behaviour would make it possible for the worker to continue working with her.

The worker recounted a pivotal incident when the manager leaned over his cubicle and criticized his work in front of his co-workers. The man had been dealing with multiple personal stressors and had serious clinical depression at the time of this incident. It had been so traumatic that any future comments the manager made about his work caused him to suffer waves of anxiety that he found very difficult to manage.

As to the manager's behaviour, the worker made a few suggestions on what could be changed. He pointed out that as the manager had an office, she had the option of offering criticism in private. He also said that it would be good to hear some positive comments and not just negative ones.

As the discussion progressed, he also shared that, especially during times when he was not well, he had a hard time understanding exactly what the manager meant by her criticism. In one instance she had said that the last two paragraphs of a report did not flow well with the rest. It would have been more productive for him if, in her feedback, she had concentrated on what she wanted done differently—in this case, that the last two paragraphs be shorter and more succinct.

Further questions and discussion failed to turn up any other problems that caused the employee's "hate" of the manager. Excessive workload did not figure in the feelings of "hate," nor unreasonable demands or pressures, nor a lack of communication—none of the usual sources of antagonism.

His complaints came from an uncomplicated incident: one day, the mental condition of a vulnerable employee who was in a sensitive state of mind, was sent into a downward spiral as a result of his manager's criticism which unintentionally triggered a chain reaction. This was then further reinforced each time the manager criticized the employee's work.

By shifting the focus away from the problem (hating the manager) to the solution (simple changes to behaviours that easily altered the interpersonal dynamics), the employee who thought he could not work with his manager any longer was able to re-establish a working relationship that years later was still going strong.

Mediation: Shuttle Diplomacy

The term shuttle diplomacy is borrowed from international relations and can be useful in sensitive workplace situations when one or more of the parties to mediation are also experiencing severe emotional distress, including mental health issues such as depression or anxiety related disorders. It refers to the use of a trusted third person who moves between stakeholders and provides each with a separate opportunity to voice concerns and engage in a discussion of solutions without having others present.

This variation on standard mediation processes recognizes that when one party is particularly vulnerable to emotional distress, the playing field is no longer level. A secure environment in which to discuss solutions can make a significant difference.

Solutions can be examined for commonalities and the outcome can be a plan that respects both parties' interests. With their dignity intact, employees come to a solution that they would otherwise have resisted if it had been imposed on them. While this approach is used to great advantage by professional mediators, it is a technique that can be employed by others who have sound interpersonal instincts.

Managing Mental Health Matters is a video-based training program that helps managers respond to emotional distress in employees. It is freely available at *workplacestrategiesformentalhealth.com.*

Involve employees in developing solutions and preventing problems

If workplaces are to recover from a poisoned work environment in a sustainable way, it's necessary for management and staff to work together and develop solutions together. The participative process that led to the solution should then become embedded in the way the organization routinely functions.

Any solution that is programmed by a third party for your staff is less likely to work.

Most people are much more committed to changes that they have had a part in—both in the development and in the implementation.

Some organizations, with the best of intentions, will invest large financial sums on 'flavour of the month' type programs. These are often experiences meant to add fun and camaraderie to the workplace and can have their benefits. But to enact a long-term improvement in morale, the best results are achieved by engaging all stakeholders—staff, management and unions where present—in developing ideas for reasonable and cost-effective solutions that they could implement together. These solutions would go beyond a single experience toward a new way of interacting and working together. Giving voice and recognition to these efforts and their outcomes helps sustain motivation and energizes the workplace community to continue their productive activities.

From victim mentality to owning the solution

We all have frustrations at work and most of us have had to work with people who irritate or annoy us. Nevertheless, we have options within our control even when we are not in charge. Managing difficult workplace dynamics can be achieved by understanding our own triggers and stressors and also by learning to negotiate relationships.

Understanding triggers and stressors

Everyone is shaped by early experiences, traumas and disappointments as well as achievements and joys. Our memories of these earlier times are often buried deep in our psyches. They shape our responses to present-day situations, often without our being aware of the source of our emotional reactions.

Many people have strong, automatic responses to a number of behaviours and traits in others. For example, they may respond without thinking to crying in others; people who won't relate to them or give them the silent treatment may drive them wild; and those with whining voices or aggressive manners may cause swift, predictable reactions. Our automatic reactions to certain behavioural traits can blind us to the reasons why we react negatively to certain people. This can be a particularly troublesome situation in the workplace if irritating behaviour is confused with poor job performance.

An example of a triggered response

Some people react strongly to passive aggressive behaviour. *Passive aggressive people appear to agree with comments and comply with requests. Instead, they will find a way to silently or passively resist while appearing to agree and throw up obstacles or challenges along the way.*

One woman describes her physical reaction to passive aggressive behaviour as typically beginning with a tightening of her facial muscles. Her jaw clenches and her blood pressure rises. She can feel anger rising up inside of her. When this happens, she has learned to deliberately and consciously take a deep breath and then exhale while reminding herself that "this person is not my father."

She has come to understand that her extreme and automatic reaction to a passive aggressive person is directly related to her experience with her passive aggressive father, who had been a constant source of frustration to her in her childhood. If she did not understand where her strong response to passive aggressive behaviour came from, she would be blaming the individual in front of her for "making" her angry, instead of recognizing that her reactions *have little to do with the situation at hand and much more to do with her own unique triggers or stressors.*

In many cases that involve long-term, problematic employee/supervisor interactions, one or both parties will often describe their emotions as having been purposely 'caused' by the other. These convictions frequently result in negative reactions that over time escalate to such a degree that there is harm to health and well-being.

Understanding the source of automatic emotional impulses will not completely eliminate the effect that triggers and stressors continue to have. Nevertheless, understanding the nature of these knee-jerk reactions—that that they are strongly coloured by unique triggers set in place by our early experiences—helps us control our impulses. By choosing the manner of our response a much more effective interaction can be achieved with people who would otherwise "push our buttons."

Learning to negotiate relationships

A fresh-start strategy that has worked in cases of employee/supervisor or co-worker conflict is to leave the old relationship behind and negotiate a new one with each other. This involves, amongst other things, making a choice to leave behind all inclination to engage in blaming and shaming the other or to dwell on who was right or who was wrong. It focuses on going forward with what two people need to work together in a professional and civil manner. They agree on a plan which allows them to take up new positive behaviours. The proviso is that each person has to commit to the new approach.

Dr. David Burns,[4] a renowned psychiatrist, once asked a large gathering of therapists to imagine the one person in their lives, either personally or through work, who most annoys them—the person who makes their life miserable, gets under their skin, and causes them grief on a regular basis.

---

[4]   See <www.feelinggood.com> for Dr. Burn's website.

"Do you have that person's face in your mind?" he asked. When everyone agreed that this despicable person was in mind, he said that he had a magic button and if pressed, that person would become your very best friend tomorrow. "Who wants to press the button?" Dr. Burns asked.

Out of about 300 participants, only a handful agreed they would press the button. The rest did not want to ever be friends with this person. Dr. Burns pointed out that many conflicting relationships, between couples, family members, co-workers or employee/supervisor, could never be fixed because one or more of the individuals just did not want it to happen.

New communication skills or relationship techniques were doomed to fail because at least one of the individuals involved had no desire to make them work. They preferred or felt justified in disliking or hating this person for the rest of their lives.

In any workplace relationship it is important to recognize that one or both parties may be unwilling to become "friends." But as long as both are willing to let go of the past and create something better for their work situation, there can still be success. At work, it often matters less whether people want to be real friends. What matters is that their behaviour towards one another remains civil. The aim is to go to work and engage with each other without negative repercussions or constant stress. What begins as a tentative or sceptical approach to engaging in a new way of interacting can become a healthy working relationship over time when each individual commits to the changes in behaviours in a plan that both helped to develop.

The skills learned through an understanding of the role of triggers and stressors in workplace environments, as well as those learned in negotiating a new relationship with managers and co-workers can also be helpful in the search for creative and effective ways to deal with the out-of-control or "toxic" boss.

"The boss from hell"

The boss was constantly berating and belittling employees. He threatened one woman that her job would be made redundant if her work was not successful. Many employees were treated in a similar fashion and he was referred to as the boss from hell.

This woman who had been threatened decided that she did not want to deal with his harassment anymore, but she valued the opportunity this job gave to her and did not want to quit. Those who had dared to complain in the past had been terminated. She began to think about why her boss might behave as he did.

She found out that he had grown up as a foster child and made an educated guess that as a result of his earlier experiences he might mistrust the motivations or intentions of others. It was also common knowledge that he had never been known to have a compassionate response and any emotional outbursts from others in the workplace were met with his disdain. He had many indisputable accomplishments, was intelligent and ambitious and possessed a strong drive to succeed, attributes that were admired by others.

After studying these observations, she deduced that her boss probably did not act from an intention to harm so much as a sense of insecurity which led him to question whether other people might be manipulating or deceiving him. He was concerned about the possibility that others might make him look bad in the eyes of his superiors or peers and desperately wanted to succeed.

She sat down with her boss and matter-of-factly asked, "How do you want the work that I am doing to reflect back on you?" Her boss looked at her for a moment and replied, "I want to get credit for being the first one to have ever made the work you do successful in the type of business that we are in." The employee was a little surprised at the boss' honesty about taking credit for her work, but responded calmly, "If I do that, and make this successful, I will have met your expectations. If I am not successful, you have made it clear that my job will be made redundant— is that correct?" When her boss said yes, the employee suggested that they strike a deal.

She explained that the humiliating comments he frequently addressed to her about the work, which he probably meant to motivate her, were having the opposite effect. If the boss was willing to stop making remarks that caused her to lose focus and would allow her to make the decisions she felt would lead to success, the employee promised to do her best so that the project would reflect well on her boss. If she failed, she would not argue with the termination of her contract. Her boss seemed momentarily taken aback by the conversation but agreed that it was a reasonable bargain.

The boss stuck by the agreement. He stopped picking on the employee and threatening her with termination. He allowed her to make her own decisions. The employee held up her end of the bargain and succeeded in achieving her goal. She had negotiated a solution that allowed each of them to move past a destructive relationship and achieve results of mutual benefit.

The employee was able to negotiate a healthier relationship for herself with her boss, but this was not an ideal resolution to a toxic environment. A skilled employee, she carved out a new way of interacting with her boss when her position was under threat of termination. Her workplace, however, remained an each-man-for-himself environment.

This employee was a canny and insightful person and was able to save her position by analyzing the underlying basis of her boss's negative interaction with her. She made a calculated guess that his anxiety about his own job and his distrust of the world around him caused him to behave in a way that had negative, potentially harmful effects on his employees. Although in this example, the particular employee found a successful solution, the boss did not necessarily become a nicer person, but it did put an end to extreme problem behaviours.

Potentially, there is legal relief for harassment, as numerous cases attest. But getting such relief can be costly, time consuming, emotionally difficult and has its own limitations. Trying to negotiate a new relationship with your boss can sometimes achieve adequate and sufficient results for you to continue working in an admittedly less than healthy environment, but it can be in each party's interest at least as a temporary solution. The success of self-help, or more accurately, self-defence solutions is limited by the fact that not everyone—probably not most people—have the skills and nerve required to carry them off.

Ultimately then, what is required is still a proactive approach on the part of employers that is based on hiring the right people to manage others.

If there is one single factor that underlies many, if not most of the cases of mental injury that find their way to courts and tribunals, it is the failure to hire and train supervisors and managers who have sound basic interpersonal skills.

Hiring, training, promoting and rewarding supervisors and managers based on the trait of interpersonal competence *in addition* to the technical or specific skills required for the job is probably the best single strategy employers can adopt in order to avoid the stress, cost and sheer misery of legal entanglements associated with claims of mental injury.

CHAPTER 5

The Psychologically Safe Workplace in Practice: The Roles of Governance, Management and Organizational Culture in Meeting Legal Requirements

From the analysis conducted in chapters 2-4 it is possible to identify some common features that must be present in any workplace that claims to be or wishes to become psychologically safe.

These features can be organized broadly under the headings of governance, management and culture.

A. Governance and Management

While this is not a treatise on governance, leadership or management as such, the law points clearly to some key aspects of these organizational functions which require attention if a psychologically safe workplace is to be achieved and sustained.

As Chart 5.1 within shows, the legal requirements for *reasonable job demands, voice and vigilance* reviewed in chapters 2-4 all have implications for governance and management.

With regard to these implications, we refer readers to a standard five element management approach to strategic planning as described by Dr. Ian M. F. Arnold, Chair of the Workforce Advisory Committee to the Mental Health Commission of Canada. The framework he describes is consistent with that used by the International Organization for Standardization (ISO) and other standard making organizations.[1]

---

[1]   See for example: British Standards Institution (BSI) PAS 1010:2010 "Guidance on the management of psychosocial risks in the workplace" (Publicly available specification. 3rd Draft v.2).

Dr. Arnold developed this framework for a forum hosted in Vancouver, B.C. by the Mental Health Commission of Canada in September 2010, the purpose of which was to identify practical strategies for the protection of psychological safety in workplaces.

The 5 Elements of a Standard Management Approach to Strategic Planning for the Psychologically Safe Workplace

(adapted from the report by the Mental Health Commission of Canada, developed with the support of the Great-West Life Centre for Mental Health in the Workplace)

Below is an explanation of the adapted framework followed by a table which places the recommendations from the 2010 Vancouver Forum within the framework.

A sustainable approach to provision of a psychologically safe workplace should include the following five briefly described elements:

1. Demonstrate Commitment:
Set Policy

Boards of Directors, CEOs, COOs, CFOs and other senior officers of the organization are called upon to commit themselves to fulfil the requirements of a psychologically safe workplace.

This commitment should be in the form of a broadly advertised statement of intent to provide a psychologically safe workplace with the same degree of diligence and application that is directed toward physical safety. Everyone should know what the organization intends. But intent is of little use unless it is translated into action. The most common vehicle for action is an institutional policy that spells out the requirements of the duty to provide a psychologically safe workplace.

The policy may call for a review and probably a revision of some existing policies because the requirements of the psychologically safe workplace need to be harmonized and made consistent with requirements of the respectful workplace, rules about harassment and discrimination and any other provisions about mental health, including how it is viewed and treated.

The provisions of the policy on the psychologically safe workplace should be commonly seen as the "headwater" from which other policies flow. It sets the tone and establishes the philosophy of how mental health is regarded by the employer.

(See draft policy and procedures in Chapter 6.)

2. Planning:
Assess where you are now and where you want to go—Define Need

Determine how employee mental health is currently supported compared to:

- Regulatory and Social Policies;

- Existing industry benchmarks.

Determine the state of employee mental health as observed through:

- Specialized individual and organizational mental health screening measures—e.g., Generalized Anxiety Disorder Questionnaire (GAD-7), Patient Health Questionnaire 9 (PHQ) and Stress Satisfaction Offset Score (SSOS);

- Assessment of organizational structural factors known to impact workplace psychological safety as found in Guarding Minds at Work: <**www.guardingmindsatwork.ca**>;

- Aggregated data (to protect individual privacy); results from sources such as:

  - E(F)AP programs;

  - Insurance records: drugs, benefits;

  - Company medical reports and voluntary health risk assessments;

  - Human resources absenteeism data;

  - Trade union—grievances, reports, records of concerns, employee relations committee;

  - Joint Health & Safety Committee proceedings, investigations or inspections;

  - Employee surveys.

3. Implementation and Operation:
Implement programs that address your organization's defined needs

Data generated by an assessment of the mental health status of an organization's workforce can be used to develop and implement cost effective programs that:

- Prevent mental injury and poor mental health;

- Address and reduce existing risk factors to mental health;

- Identify and provide assistance to those employees experiencing early concerns about mental health issues.

Workplace primary prevention programs might include:

- Confidential health risk assessments, including the provision of referral advice;

- Safe return to work programs that acknowledge the vulnerability of returning workers to psychological injury;

- Stress management programs;

- Management and workforce training programs.

Programs that address workforce needs can include:

- Facilitated access to professional advice;

- Training of designated peer supporters;

- Flexible work scheduling practices;

- Appointment of safe workplace advocates;

- Union representation and consultation in addressing needs;

- Job-Share programs.

Programs that address existing mental health issues:

- Training of management to identify and approach employees who may be struggling;

- Effective accommodation and return-to-work practices that acknowledge the hyper-vulnerability of workers attempting return to work after an episode of mental disability;

- Peer support programs (e.g., Alcoholics Anonymous, Post-traumatic Stress Disorder peer support).

4. Review and Corrective Action

A review function evaluates at regular intervals how well the organization is meeting its goals for a psychologically safe workplace—no less than twice a year. Information from this process ensures continual quality improvement in repetitive cycles. This process usually involves the repeated use of measurements of the sort described under "Planning" above.

5. Accountability

Unless one or more senior managers reporting to the CEO, COO or owner has responsibility within their job descriptions for the development and maintenance of a psychologically safe workplace, it is extremely unlikely that the desired conditions will be achieved. Accountability and review functions with regard to achievement and sustainability of the psychologically safe workplace must be part of the core operating procedures of the organization.

Psychological safety is a key piece of the business plan—it describes a way of conducting business that puts a high priority on protecting the mental health of its workers. For this reason, planning and progress reports concerning the development and maintenance of a psychologically safe workplace are of central importance in any organization's accountability system.

The specific recommendations of participants at the Vancouver Forum on the Psychologically Safe Workplace can be fitted to the Five Element approach just described as follows:

The 5 Elements Showing Forum Participant Recommendations According to Stages of Employment and Organizational Functions

	Commitment and Policy	Planning	Implementation and Operation	Review and Corrective Actions	Accountability
Recruiting and Hiring	Define "psychologically safe workplace" for new recruits. Articulate the values of Organization and how they will be upheld or measured. State that no negligent, reckless or intentional injury to employee mental health is tolerated or condoned.	Consider Emotional Intelligence in selection and promotion of those whose role involves supervision or support of employees. Ensure the hiring process includes consideration of psychological safety for interviewees.	Discuss accommodation and organizational supports as well as the process to obtain assistance in the workplace. Define cultural and social expectations or norms within your workplace. Increase psychological comfort by considering recruiting options such as: - sharing the interview process in advance; - providing written questions at the time of interview; - offering a choice of sequential vs. panel interviews.	3-6 month review of job-fit to assess the effectiveness of recruiting and hiring practices. Measure satisfaction and engagement as well as performance. Consider a short survey asking about the recruiting and hiring process to seek input for improvement. If necessary provide relevant training and support. If changes are needed review again in another 3-6 months as necessary.	Annual Review of recruiting and hiring practices overall and analysis of the outcomes.

	Commitment and Policy	Planning	Implementation and Operation	Review and Corrective Actions	Accountability
Orientation and Training	Require that the Organization Values be embedded in both orientation and all training approaches.	Consider how all (or the absence of) orientation and training processes may impact psychological safety.	Define an orientation program that takes into account mental health aspects of the job, the culture, rates of change within the organization, application of organizational values, how to access support or accommodation. Set up a management development process that includes awareness of mental health and mental illness, development of interpersonal competence, access to just-in-time resources, and coaching/coaching/mentoring. Set up a shorter orientation process for job changes within the organization.	Require all training and orientation to be assessed for impact on behavior of the trainee and others, as well as outcomes. Ask what challenges there were in new job placement to learn how to improve orientation and training approaches. Ask about training requirements and training refreshers to understand the needs.	Do scheduled reviews of organization-wide, department and job-specific orientation and training approaches and compare to other measures of psychological safety and engagement.

	Commitment and Policy	Planning	Implementation and Operation	Review and Corrective Actions	Accountability
Evaluation, performance management, discipline and promotion	Require senior leaders and those responsible for governance to "walk the talk" of organizational values.	Develop a system that supports psychological safety in the approach to management, evaluation, discipline and promotion.	Ensure those responsible for management of people have a minimum standard of emotional intelligence or support to develop this skill. Create a performance management system that rules out health problems before beginning discipline and embeds solution-focused approaches in working with employee issues. Engage employees in developing solutions that allow them to accomplish the tasks assigned. Help supervisors and managers to identify and solve workplace issues promptly and in a sustainable manner.	Take regular account of productivity by measuring outcomes rather than outputs (i.e., measure results rather than effort such as showing up every day or working longer hours). Analyze external influences on performance such as economic pressures, family issues, community disasters, as well as employee conflict, and organizational pressures.	Consider the impact of the various systems of management and evaluation and whether they result in desired outcomes. Consider pilot projects to test out alternative approaches.

	Commitment and Policy	Planning	Implementation and Operation	Review and Corrective Actions	Accountability
Intervention and Crisis Response	Require clear standards of response in the event of crisis.	Ensure that crisis response programs include aspects related to those with mental health concerns as well as considering the psychological impact of a crisis on all employees.	Develop programs for proactive crisis prevention. Develop intervention programs to assist troubled employees. EAP programs must be relevant to your org.	Assess efficacy of programs and relevance to need.	Review all programs, look for synergies, and consider gaps.
Accommodation and Return to Work	Ensure understanding of and compliance with Human Rights and Disability Law.	Define accommodation opportunities that address issues related to communication, feedback, directions, relationships, triggers and stressors in the workplace as well as task oriented approaches. Consider the impact on others during accommodation and return to work planning.	Create a return to work process that includes consideration of psychological impacts, even for those returning after physical injuries or illness. Consider refresher or new training for anyone who has been away for 2 months or more, or during a time of change in processes or procedures.	Have regular follow-up for at least the first 6 months of a return to work. Have at least annual follow-up for accommodation to ensure it is still the most effective solution making sure that needs are being met.	Review annually against human rights or disability law changes and for effectiveness from the perspective of employee and supervisor. Make changes as needed.

	Commitment and Policy	Planning	Implementation and Operation	Review and Corrective Actions	Accountability
Accommodation and Return to Work *cont.*		Proactively remove or reduce barriers to work related to psychological safety and support.	Develop an accommodation approach that engages the employee fully in finding solutions and that allows them to be successful at their job. Support supervisors in understanding and sustaining all aspects of a successful return to work including changes in communication and feedback.		
Redeployment and Termination	Ensure leaders are physically present and communicate effectively during times of layoff or redeployment.	Explore community resources, organizational or benefit provider resources and external providers for approaches and supports available to those who are losing their jobs.	Provide targeted training programs for those managing organizational change and those who execute terminations.	Solicit feedback from both those who are let go (exit interviews) and those left behind about the perception of the company response to layoff or redeployment.	Prepare for possible future situations by having plans in place or consider next steps if the event has already occurred.

	Commitment and Policy	Planning	Implementation and Operation	Review and Corrective Actions	Accountability
Redeployment and Termination *cont.*		Consider the psychological impact on 'survivors' of downsizing, layoffs or redeployments. In times of significant change consider the psychological impact of job insecurity, lack of role clarity, competition or collaboration with newcomers, changing or unclear expectations or values.	Ensure availability of resources to support the employee in dealing with the emotional fallout and subsequent job search. Consider the needs of those who may have mental health issues at the time of termination and the psychological safety of those who are terminating.		
Organizational Structure	Consider the potential psychological impact from style of governance, new development approaches and existing organizational structures. Require integration of psychological safety in existing and future programs.	Collect data that will help guide the development or evolution of the organizational structure including focus on psychological impact. Analyze data and involve stakeholders in developing alternative approaches.	Ensure psychological safety for all positions including those that utilize non-standard approaches such as telecommuting, working alone and other flexible work arrangements.	Audit of all programs to ensure that psychological factors are measured and addressed at regular intervals.	Review results using continuous improvement framework.

	Commitment and Policy	Planning	Implementation and Operation	Review and Corrective Actions	Accountability
Organizational Structure *cont.*		Consider the psychological impact of communication and feedback loops, job security, role clarity, levels of competition and collaboration, clarity of expectations, values and policies.			
Job Design	Organizational policy to include a process to assess healthy and safe job design—e.g., job risk assessment and cognitive demands analysis.	Plan/review jobs to ensure that psychological demands are assessed and psychological safety is addressed.	Job design for those in supervisory or management positions includes adequate time to provide a psychologically safe work environment.	Seek feedback from those in the jobs to assess if the design is psychologically safe and clearly defined. Make adjustments as necessary.	Review job design when new jobs are developed or there are significant changes to jobs.

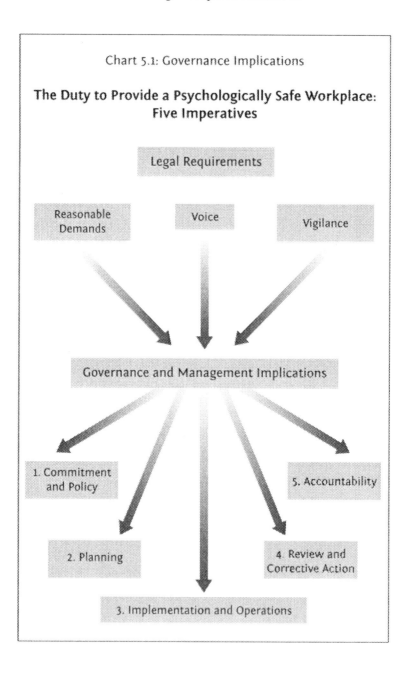

Chart 5.1: Governance Implications

The Duty to Provide a Psychologically Safe Workplace: Five Imperatives

Legal Requirements

Reasonable Demands

Voice

Vigilance

Governance and Management Implications

1. Commitment and Policy

5. Accountability

2. Planning

4. Review and Corrective Action

3. Implementation and Operations

1. Reasonable Demands.

Keep job demands reasonable and adjust them to individual capacities. Employers are responsible for determining what excessive and unreasonable demands mean in relation to individual employees and for taking appropriate steps to adjust the situation where required.

2. Voice.

Make it safe to speak up. There is a responsibility to create an atmosphere of basic trust in which workers who report to you or for whom you have obligations feel safe in declaring problematic situations, circumstances and conditions which are affecting, or might affect their job performance. This includes the responsibility to learn about critical vulnerabilities among your workers.

3. Vigilance.

Monitor and respond to warning signs of conflict among workers. Employers must be aware of, and take proactive steps to amend situations of interpersonal conflict that could foreseeably give rise to mental injury. This includes the responsibility to appoint supervisors and managers who meet a floor standard of interpersonal competence (aka "emotional intelligence").

Assistance in converting the requirements of a psychologically safe workplace into governance and management practices can be found in a free, web-based resource called Guarding Minds at Work, available in English and in French <www.guardingmindsatwork.ca>. Employers can acquaint themselves with the fundamental concept and requirements of the psychologically safe workplace and use Guarding Minds at Work as a strategy for assessing and addressing risks to mental health that are embedded in the ways in which work is designed, managed and supervised.

The strategy was developed by a team of researcher-practitioners at Simon Fraser University and was funded by Great-West Life's Centre for Mental Health in the Workplace.

After providing a comprehensive rationale for why employers should be interested in psychological safety, Guarding Minds at Work moves on to practical methods for assessing and addressing risks to mental health. Among the tools provided are: an Audit, a short (6 item) survey called the Initial Scan (or SSIX) and a longer survey called the PSR 12 or psychosocial risk inventory.

Among other things, users will find helpful advice on how to assemble the right people to undertake key tasks, how to communicate the purpose and methodology of the process and how to implement it as a participative process.

The philosophy of Guarding Minds at Work is that the process of planning and implementation should be as health promoting in itself as the outcome: the process (properly carried out) is part of the solution. Readers are encouraged to visit the site and to consider its use as a means of implementing in particular the third key legal requirement of a psychologically safe workplace: the need to exercise vigilance.

As a result of pointing to areas of strength and weakness through the exercise of vigilance, the assessment process also draws attention to the ways in which the other two legal responsibilities (reasonable demands and voice) are being discharged within the organization.

But this exercise will very likely lead to the realization that there are aspects of the *culture* of the organization that need attention. And it is to this project that we now turn.

B. Culture

The strategic initiatives outlined under governance and management are necessary, but not sufficient for the achievement of a psychologically safe workplace. Unless the broad principles of psychological safety are translated into cultural realities on a day-to-day basis they will remain like so much corporate graffiti on the boardroom wall.

What methods can be used to effect or facilitate this translation?

Revisiting the analyses conducted in chapters 2-4, certain common themes emerge that direct our attention toward what needs to be done to achieve psychologically safe *workplace cultures*.

A workplace culture is defined for these purposes as a set of shared values, attitudes and understandings characteristic of a group, department, unit, team or organization.

What does the law have to say about the key qualities or conditions of a workplace culture that is supportive of psychological safety?

And what can we deduce about psychologically safe workplace cultures from the alternate stories where different endings have been proposed or suggested for the cases in chapters 2-4?

In other words, what conditions support *reasonable demands, voice and vigilance* as we have defined them?

If these fundamental responsibilities that form the basis of the duty to provide a psychologically safe workplace are used as a lens through which to view the workplace, an answer begins to emerge.

Three main conditions play prominent roles. They have been identified as a result of observed convergences between the directions suggested by the law, by the proven success of interventions that changed the course of otherwise toxic situations, and by our own and others' studies of an innovative team based intervention.[2]

When the three following conditions exist **as the norm**, it can be said with confidence that a psychologically safe situation exists:

1. **Awareness**: prevails when there is a high level of awareness among team or work unit members of *who* is influenced by their words and actions and *how* they are influenced.

2. **Understanding**: prevails when there is a high level of understanding among team or work unit members of the legitimate needs, interests, motives and points of view of others.

3. **Carefulness**: prevails when team or work unit members habitually act upon their awareness and understanding by taking all reasonable precautions to avoid doing foreseeable harm to one another.

Collectively the conditions are known as the "**Neighbour at Work**" principles.[3]

---

[2] **Vital Workplace** is a prototype that has been tested in several workplace environments with encouraging results. While it is true that many team based interventions exist, the challenge is to use or adapt them to focus on the three conditions or principles described here: awareness, understanding and carefulness. Vital Workplace was conceived and designed to achieve this purpose. The key elements can be found on the Neighbour at Work website <www.neighbouratwork.com>. The purpose of this demonstration is to help employers understand what is required of a cultural intervention if it is to achieve higher levels of psychological safety. Once understood, employers can negotiate with whoever provides or might provide such services for inclusion of these key elements.

[3] See <www.neighbouratwork.com> for details.

The three legal requirements—Reasonable Demands, Voice, and Vigilance—dovetail with Awareness, Understanding and Carefulness in the manner shown on the following diagram

Requirements of the legal duty to provide a psychologically safe workplace	Neighbour at Work Imperatives		
	Awareness	Understanding	Carefulness
Reasonable Demands	✓✓✓	✓✓	✓
Voice	✓✓	✓✓✓	✓
Vigilance	✓	✓✓	✓✓✓

All three Neighbour at Work imperatives are important to the fulfillment of *all three* legal requirements, but the number of checkmarks in the table above demonstrates different degrees of emphasis.

For example, ensuring that the job demands you make of a worker are not taking too high a toll on their mental health depends in large measure on the extent to which you have an awareness of how you affect that person.

Similarly, the facilitation of voice (in this context, feeling it is safe to declare or reveal personal concerns or problems) is of cardinal importance to the likelihood that members of a team will be able to recognize and accommodate one another's interests and rights up to a reasonable standard.

And vigilance on everyone's part is clearly required in order to achieve a norm of carefulness, which is to say, the avoidance of reasonably foreseeable harm.

Diving Deeper

If we seek an even more fundamental basis for a psychologically safe workplace culture, we must take a closer look at the *emotional heart* of the employment relationship, namely the *promises* that bind the parties together in a contractual undertaking.

The language of emotions and promises may sound paradoxical, even quixotic in a legal context. One might expect the law to deal in hard facts and to shun all talk of emotions. But at least some of the cases reviewed in chapters 2-4 reveal that judges, commissioners and arbitrators can get quite emotional themselves sometimes as they try to sort out the messes that workplace actors bring before them for resolution.

What judges, commissioners and arbitrators are so often talking about in their decisions is the fact that the actors *did not keep their promises to one another*—those implied and sometimes explicit promises of the employment relationship.

When we say "to one another," we include everyone. "One another" is not code for "the bad employer broke his or her promise": in many cases neither party behaved very well, at least in terms of honouring their promises.

Since promises are the emotional heart of the employment contract, it is here that we must look for the fundamental dynamic that minimizes conflict in the employment relationship and drastically reduces the likelihood of spawning legal issues associated with mental injury.

This being the case, a useful way of looking at the *key requirements* of the duty to provide a psychologically safe workplace is to see them as reflections of the *key promises* of the employment relationship. When employers make reasonable demands, facilitate employee voice, and are vigilant for signs of dissention and conflict, they are keeping core promises of the employment relationship.

In turn, the honouring of these core promises goes a long way toward creating a fertile environment for *awareness, understanding and carefulness*, the conditions that need to be present in high functioning teams and work units.

We have learned quite a lot about the keeping of promises. Promises are more likely to be kept if they meet certain criteria.[4] If from the outset they are:

■ reasonable (practical, doable) for both parties;

■ clear and unambiguous;

■ freely made and not coerced;

■ based on information symmetry (both parties have the same information);

■ frequently revisited and "maintained";

… they stand the best chance of being honoured.

Knowing this about promises has implications for all stages and phases of the employment relationship. If these principles are followed during the hiring process and also during assessment and review for promotion, in the course of performance evaluations, and while employees are in the process of returning to work after episodes of illness or debilitation,

---

[4] T.E. Tyler et al, *Social justice in a diverse society* (Oxford, UK: Westview, 1997); M.J. Trebilcock, *The Limits of Freedom of Contract* (Cambridge, MA: Harvard University Press, 1997); J.E. Ferrie et al, "Injustice at work and incidence of psychiatric morbidity: the Whitehall 2 study" (2006) 63 Occupational and Environmental Medicine 443-450; M. Elovainio et al, "Organisational justice and impaired cardiovascular regulation among female employees" (2006) 63 Occupational and Environmental Medicine 141-144.

the odds are raised in favour of establishing or re-establishing the relationship on a stable and harmonious basis.

Finally, since managers and supervisors are particularly important in creating workplace culture, they need to understand that their approach to the honouring of promises is crucial.

What managerial and supervisory attitudes and practices are likely to contribute to honouring promises?

The evidence all points to a "balanced expressive/directive style of management."[5]

At its core this is a style that is:

- communicative,

- supportive,

- participative,

- cooperative.

---

[5] M. Buckingham and C. Coffman, *First, break all the Rules: what the world's greatest managers do differently* (New York, NY: Simon and Schuster, 1999); A.J. DuBrin, *Essentials of Management* (Cincinnati, OH: South-Western, 1990); J.J. Goldman, "The Supervisor's Beliefs about People and the Supervisory Plan: McGregor's "Theory X" and "Theory Y" in the Schools" (1983) The Clearing House (March) 306(4); W. Ouchi, *Theory Z: how American Management can meet the Japanese Challenge* (Reading, MA: Addison-Wesley, 1981); P.J. Frost, *Toxic Emotions at Work. How Compassionate Managers Handle Pain and Conflict* (Boston, MA: Harvard Business School Press, 2003); I.M. Nembhard and A.C. Edmondson, "Making it safe: the effects of leader inclusiveness and professional status on psychological safety and improvement efforts in health care teams" (2006) Journal of Organizational Behavior 27(7) at 941-966; J.R. Detertand and E.R. Burris, "Leadership behavior and employee voice: Is the door really open?" (2007) 50 Academy of Management Journal 4 at 869-884; F.O. Walumbwa and J. Schaubroeck, "Leader personality traits and employee voice behavior: Mediating roles of ethical leadership and work group psychological safety" (2009) 94 Journal of Applied Psychology 5 at 1275-1286; A. Carmeli, D. Brueller and J.E. Dutton, "Learning behaviours in the workplace: The role of high-quality interpersonal relationships and psychological safety" (2009) 26 Systems Research and Behavioral Science 1 at 81-98.

While also being, when needed:

- decisive,

- directive.

The key to the balance between the expressive elements (the first four) and the directive elements (the last two) appears to be an ability to involve staff in a division of labour that they understand and to which they actively consent.

Expressive skills are essential to making the group process work when roles and responsibilities are discussed, understood and fairly distributed within the work group. These skills are a subset to those that define emotional intelligence or EI.[6]

The key skills or capacities of EI relevant to management style are:

- **Self-Awareness**: being aware of your own feelings and of how you affect others in your circle of influence.

- **Awareness of Others**: being conscious of the interests, needs, strengths, and limitations of others and of how they affect you.

- **Self-Expression**: being able to express what you feel, say what you mean, and mean what you say.

- **Relationship Management**: knowing how to manage and defuse conflict, motivate others, and help others to develop through guidance, coaching, and mentoring.

Note the similarity between these attributes and skills and the Neighbour at Work principles described earlier. This similarity is no accident,

---

[6]   D. Goleman, *Emotional Intelligence* (New York, NY: Bantam Books, 1995); D. Goleman, *Working with Emotional Intelligence* (New York, NY: Bantam Books, 1998).

because every member of a team or work group needs some of the same skills as the people who manage them, although perhaps not always to the same degree.

EI is neither a substitute for other types of intelligence, nor for the directive skills that every good leader must possess. Nevertheless EI can help leaders understand *when and how* those directive skills can and should be used.

EI helps leaders negotiate and maintain an equitable division of labour in their work group. The process of deciding what tasks are to be performed, by whom, by when, and how, has an important effect on the fairness with which they are perceived.

Perhaps the best prescription for building a psychologically safe workplace culture, as a priority, is the need to refine and build on the skills acquired through emotional intelligence.

Recruitment, training, promotion and evaluation of employee performance using the additional criterion of emotional intelligence, over time, can be expected to have a significantly positive impact on the psychological safety of *any* working environment, in whatever sector of the economy and in organizations of all sizes.

CHAPTER 6

Near Horizons: Creating National Standards for the
Psychologically Safe Workplace

The stories of human suffering and loss that were drawn upon for chapters 2-4 illustrate beyond a doubt that the impact of mental injury at work does not stay in the workplace, but rather migrates out into families, communities and society as a whole as a form of social exhaust.

While we do not know the exact financial impact of this migration, preliminary efforts to quantify it place it in the realm of $33 billion a year in Canada alone.[1]

This impact is felt in key systems of our society: health care, social services, even corrections.

It impacts in ways that are too difficult to measure: how families function, the vibrancy of communities and neighbourhoods, how often people participate in political affairs. It is reflected in how much money people have to spend with predictable results in the economy as a whole.

This phenomenon of harm migration identifies the psychologically safe workplace as a social as well as a corporate challenge. It strongly suggests a need to identify the protection of mental health in the workplace as a population health issue—one that is addressed at a national policy level.

One very important way in which national initiatives can support individual employers is through the development and dissemination of *national standards* for the assessment and abatement of risks to the mental health of workers.

---

[1]　See references at <www.workplacestrategiesformentalhealth.com>.

Presently, efforts are underway in Canada to forge one or more such standards to help employers understand and act upon their legal duty to provide a psychologically safe and healthy workplace.

Such standards emerge at a time when employers are under pressure from many sources to do a better job of protecting the mental health of their employees.

It is not possible at this moment in time to describe the exact content of the standards because they have not been developed yet, but it is possible to outline what they *must* contain if they are to help employers address the three major legal requirements that formed the content of chapters 2-4.

It is possible that the standards will go *beyond* the legal requirements to also provide practical guidance on how the workplace can become more psychologically *healthy* as well as more psychologically *safe*.

Our position is that safety comes before health: indeed, it is a prerequisite for health. That said, it is worthwhile examining the whole framework which includes safety *and* health so that a holistic vision of what is called for in a psychologically safe and healthy workplace can be viewed.

For that reason the draft standards proposed here include both dimensions, but we highlight the "must do's" so they can be differentiated from the "nice to do's."

A standard in this context can be defined as a uniform method of conceptualizing, planning, executing and evaluating a strategy for a psychologically safe workplace.

The conceptualization of the strategy calls for an organizational policy from which all the other elements flow.

Consequently, the following contains a draft of both a generic social policy statement and a set of standards related to it.

Hopefully, these will serve to facilitate further discussion of the need for the fuller protection of mental health at work.

They can be used as *templates* for adaptation to a variety of organizational conditions.

Preamble to the Policy[2]

We know that certain ways of organizing and managing work can present risks to the mental health of employees.

This policy is concerned only with those ***significant*** risks associated with organizing and managing work that are ***within the power of employers to modify***.

In many cases these risks can be identified and abated, much like risks in the physical environment.

According to both scientific and legal evidence, organizational and managerial practices presenting risks to employee mental health include, but are not limited to the ***chronic and consistent***:

- **Imposition of unreasonable or excessive job demands *["Demands"]*.**[3]

- **Withholding of adequate levels of materially important information, whether by choice or neglect *["Information"]*.**

---

[2]   This policy is intended as a foundation document in so far as others relating to mental health should be consistent with it, and flow from it.

[3]   Bolded items refer to areas that, as we have seen in chapters 2-4, tend to give rise to legal issues.

- Refusal to allow the exercise of reasonable personal discretion over the day-to-day means, manner and methods of work *["**Personal Discretion**"]*.

- Failure to acknowledge or credit contributions and achievements *["**Reward**"]*.

- Failure to support others in their work through timely counsel, direction, advice and provision of basic resources to get the job done *["**Support**"]*.

- Failure to recognize and acknowledge the legitimate claims, interests and rights of others, particularly those involving dignity, integrity of the person and privacy *["**Fairness**"]*.

Accordingly, we will aim for a workplace in which, to the extent practical, our employees will experience:

- Job demands that are maintained at a reasonable level most of the time;

- Supply of important information in a timely and complete manner;

- Reasonable levels of discretion, consistent with the nature of their work, over how they do their jobs;

- Adequate acknowledgment for their contributions in terms of credit and recognition;

- Personal support by supervisors with regard to advice, direction, planning and provision of technical and practical resources to the extent that they are available within the organization;

- Recognition and reasonable accommodation of their legitimate interests, claims and rights by others.

The Policy (draft language for adaptation by specific employers)

This organization undertakes to support and protect mental health at work by all reasonable and practical means available.

For these purposes we define a psychologically safe workplace as one that makes every reasonable effort to protect the mental health of employees.

Our eventual aim is a "zero mental injury workplace".

The pursuit and achievement of a psychologically safe workplace is an article of sound business practice and we declare our intention to provide and maintain such a workplace by following the standards and procedures described below.

Proposed Floor Standards and Procedures for the Protection of Mental Health at Work

We will provide and maintain a psychologically safe workplace to the extent possible by following the procedures listed below.

These procedures address the ***measurement and abatement*** of hazards to mental health according to ***a set of evidence-based standards***.

(a) Information will be collected within this workplace on at least an annual basis concerning the prevalence of psychosocial hazards seen as arising from organizational practices and their perceived impact on mental health using as a minimum the questions under ***"Proposed Floor Standards for Assessing a Psychologically Safe Workplace"*** below.

(b) The focus in this regard is on the dimensions of demand, information adequacy, exercise of discretion, psychological rewards, support and procedural fairness.[4]

(c) Decision rules or criteria will be established for determining at what point action must be taken to abate identified psychosocial hazards related to unacceptable levels of demand, information adequacy, discretion, psychological rewards, support and procedural fairness. [A set of *proposed measurement standards* is given below to provide a point of departure for establishing these rules.]

(d) Scientifically valid and reliable instruments will be used for this purpose.

(e) Commitment from Senior Management to act on the results of such surveys will be given clearly and without ambiguity.

(f) The process described in points "a to d" forms part of the central accountability procedures of the organization so that it is overseen and invigilated by at least one senior officer who reports to the CEO and whose job description includes this function.

(g) There is a related commitment to monitor and invigilate the process as it unfolds and to modify it as needed.

(h) The duty of diligence outlined above regarding information collection and use as it bears upon the prevalence of psychosocial hazards is explicitly linked to the organization's Occupational Health and Safety surveillance and monitoring system.

(i) Adequate financial resources will be allocated to the pursuit of this process through a dedicated cost centre under the control of a senior executive.

---

[4] These dimensions are consistent with those contained in the emerging UK standards as discussed in chapter 5, but place a greater emphasis on procedural fairness. This emphasis is a result of recent studies that consistently point to the central importance of this dimension.

Proposed Floor Standards for Assessing a Psychologically Safe Workplace

The questions below are drawn from the PSR 12, which is a survey used in the assessment phase of Guarding Minds at Work. <www. guardingmindsatwork.ca>

When used as the basis for establishing that a workplace is operating at or above a floor standard of psychological safety, 85% *or more* of the workforce would *agree or strongly agree* with the following statements; and/or

15% *or less* of the workforce would *disagree or strongly disagree* with the following statements:

Demands

1. The amount of work I am expected to do is reasonable for my position.

Information

2. I am informed about important changes at work before they happen.

Personal Discretion

3. I am satisfied with the amount of involvement I have in decisions that affect my work.

Reward

4. I feel I am well rewarded (in terms of praise and recognition) for the level of effort I put out for my job.

Support

5. My supervisor supports me in getting my work done.

Fairness

6. I am satisfied with the fairness and respect I receive on the job.

Should an organization discover that it does not meet the floor standard as defined above, it is encouraged to use the Guarding Minds at Work process in order to learn more about options for assessing and addressing the psychosocial hazards intimated by this survey.

INDEX